STRATEGIES
for Content Area
READING

LEVEL
C

- **Primary Sources**
- **Science and Math Content**
- **Study Skills**
- **Content Vocabulary**
- **Test Preparation**

Options
Publishing Inc.

Table of Contents

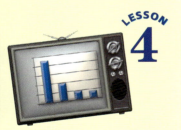

Math Connection

Product Development: Atlantic Group, Christine Lund Orciuch
Design and Production: The Quarasan Group, Inc.
Reviewer: John-Paul Bianchi, Social Studies Supervisor, New York City Board of Education
Editor: Carolyn Thresher
Production Supervisor: Sandy Batista
Cover Design: Alan Lee

Abbreviations are as follows: t=top, c=center, b=bottom, l=left, r=right

Photography Credits:
Page 2 (b) ©Corbis; 3 (br) ©MetaTools, (cr) ©PhotoDisc, Inc., (tl) ©Courtesy of NASA; 5 border ©Corel, ©Stuart Westmorland/Getty Images; 6 ©Doug Mazell/Index Stock Imagery/PictureQuest; 7 ©Ann Purcell, Carl Purcell/Words & Pictures/PictureQuest; 8 ©Myron Brenton/Omni-Photo Communications; 9 ©Johann Schumacher; 10 ©Stuart Westmorland/Getty Images; 11 ©Gerald Cubitt; 12 ©Corbis; 13 ©Comstock, Inc.; 14 ©Wolfgang Kaehler/Corbis; 17 border ©Cartesia, ©Cartesia; 22 ©Joe Atlas/Artville; 24 (t) ©Corbis, (c) ©Corbis, (b) ©Corbis; 25 (tl) ©Corbis, (bl) ©Corbis, (tr) ©Uwe Walz/Corbis, (br) ©Corbis; 29 border ©Gianni Dagli Orti/Corbis, ©Gianni Dagli Orti/Corbis; 30 ©Gianni Dagli Orti/Corbis; 31 ©Collection Roger-Viollet/Getty Images; 32 ©Nik Wheeler/Corbis; 34 ©Gianni Dagli Orti/Corbis; 37 ©Photodisc, Inc.; 38 ©Nik Wheeler/Corbis; 39 ©Nik Wheeler/Corbis; 40 ©Collection Roger-Viollet/Getty Images; 47 ©MetaTools; 50 ©PhotoDisc, Inc.; 51 ©PhotoDisc, Inc.; 52 ©PhotoDisc, Inc.; 53 ©PhotoDisc, Inc.; 54 ©PhotoDisc, Inc.; 57 ©Yann Arthus-Bertrand/Corbis; 58 ©Yann Arthus-Bertrand/Corbis; 59 ©Jim Erickson/Corbis; 60 ©Gary Braasch/Corbis; 61 (l) ©Wolfgang Kaehler/Corbis; (r) ©Sandro Vannini/Corbis; 63 ©Yann Arthus-Bertrand/Corbis; 64 ©Corbis; 65 border ©Robert Essel NYC/Corbis, ©PhotoDisc, Inc.; 66 ©Cartesia; 67 ©Michael S. Yamashita/Corbis; 68 ©Domn Smetzer/PhotoEdit, Inc.; 69 ©Tom Wagner/Corbis Saba; 70 ©Vince Streano/Corbis; 71 ©Michael S. Yamashita/Corbis; 72 ©Asian Art & Archaeology, Inc./Corbis; 73 ©Annebicque Bernard/Corbis Sygma; 74 (l) ©Vince Streano/Corbis, (r) ©Michael S. Yamashita/Corbis; 75 (l) ©Tom Carter/PhotoEdit, Inc., (r) ©Michael Freeman/Corbis; 77 border ©Courtesy of NASA, ©Corbis; 78 ©PhotoDisc, Inc.; 79 ©Courtesy of NASA; 80 ©Courtesy of NASA; 84 ©Gary Schultz; 86 ©Corbis; 88 ©Alaska Stock Images; 89 border ©PhotoDisc, Inc.; ©Reuters NewMedia Inc./Corbis; 90 ©PhotoDisc, Inc.; 91 ©Dorling Kindersley Picture Library; 92 ©Ariel Skelley/Corbis; 93 ©Dorling Kindersley Picture Library; 94-95 ©David Young-Wolff/PhotoEdit, Inc.; 96 ©Robert Landau/Corbis; 97 ©Peter Turnley/Corbis; 98 ©Horace Bristol/Corbis; 99 ©PhotoDisc, Inc.; 101 border ©MetaTools; ©PhotoDisc, Inc.; 102 ©Corbis; 103 ©KJ Historical/Corbis; 104 ©PhotoDisc, Inc.; 105 ©Historical Picture Archive/Corbis; 107 ©Corbis; 109 ©Stapleton Collection/Corbis; 111 (l) ©Stuart Westmorland/Corbis, (r) ©Michael S. Yamashita/Corbis; 112 ©Philip Gould/Corbis; 113 border ©Getty Images, ©Digital Vision/PictureQuest; 114 ©Burke/Triolo/Brand X Pictures/PictureQuest; 117 ©Digital Vision/PictureQuest; 118 ©E.S. Ross/Visuals Unlimited, Inc.; 122 ©Image Ideas, Inc./PictureQuest; 124 (t) ©MetaTools, (b) ©MetaTools; 126 ©Cartesia; 127 ©Gary Schultz; 131 ©Richard Bickel/Corbis; 132 ©PhotoDisc, Inc.; 136 ©Corbis; 137 ©Wolfgang Keahler/Corbis; 138 (l) ©Marc Garanger/Corbis, (r) ©Staffan Widstrand/Corbis; 139 ©Staffan Widstrand/Corbis.

Illustration Credits:
Page 2 (t), 36, 46, 71 Cecile Duray-Bito; 3 (bl), 115, 116, 119, 120, 134 Ka Botzis; 18 George Ladas; 19, 20–21, 23, 24–25, 27, 28, 33, 55, 85, 133 Gary Antonetti; 81, 82, 83 Michael DiGiorgio.

ISBN-10: 1-59137-028-0
ISBN-13: 978-1-59137-028-4

Options Publishing Inc.
P.O. Box 1749
Merrimack, NH 03054-1749
TOLL FREE: 800-782-7300 FAX: 866-424-4056
www.optionspublishing.com

People and Their Environments

The environment (en-VYE-ruhn-muhnt) is the natural world of land, sea, and air. The environment shapes how people travel, the kinds of houses they live in, and even the type of food they eat. Because environments are different, people have different ways of living. How does your environment shape the way you live?

Think About Cause and Effect

When you look for reasons why things happen, you are looking for causes and effects. The **cause** of an event is the reason something happens. What happens as a result is the **effect**. For example:

Cause	Effect
Because it snows a lot where I live,	our town has many snowplows.

To find cause and effect, follow these tips:

- Ask what happened.
- Ask why it happened. This is the cause.
- The cause makes the effect happen.

Think About the Topic

Reread the paragraph at the top of the page. A cause is listed below. Write the effect on the lines below.

Cause: Because environments are different,

Effect: _____

_____

_____

_____

LESSON 1
Understanding Cause and Effect

STRATEGIES•TEST PREP
Question
Understand Cause and Effect
Draw Conclusions
Compare and Contrast
Use Study Skills

People and Their Environments

If you lived in the desert, how would you travel from place to place? Could you use a bicycle? What if you lived in a cold place covered with snow? How would you travel if you lived there?

Where people live decides the way they move from place to place. When most people think of travel, they think of using cars or buses. Yet in certain places, cars are not the best way to travel.

Some cities in the world are built on very wet land. Because there is so much water, people use boats. Venice, Italy, is built on wet, soggy land. Instead of streets, there are canals. These canals look like small rivers running throughout the city. See the photograph of the canals at the top of this page. People use boats to get from place to place. Even the taxis and public buses are boats.

Question

As you read "People and Their Environments," think about what you already know about the topic. This will help you understand more about causes and effects in the article.

✏️ **WRITE HERE**

The author tells you that where people live decides the way they travel.

Cause: Because Venice is built on wet, soggy land,

Effect: _____

_____

© 2003 Options Publishing Inc.

People will always need to travel. Where they live often decides how they travel. People learn to adapt, or change, to make the most of their environment.

In places very far north, like Alaska and parts of northern Canada, people use snowshoes to help them walk over the snow. Since the mountains in some parts of Asia are very steep, cars cannot travel the narrow roads. The people use an animal called a yak. It carries people and goods from place to place.

Bicycles are important in many large cities. They are easier to use on the crowded city streets. In some Asian cities, bicycles are used as taxis.

How do people travel in the desert? Some deserts have miles of deep, soft sand. As a result, in Africa and Australia, many people still use camels. Because a camel has wide hooves, it does not sink into the sand. It can move easily over the sand.

A water buffalo carries a young boy in the Philippines.

Understand Cause and Effect

Authors often use cause and effect to help the reader understand why things happen. Look for the **cause** as you read. Ask *why* the event happens. Look for clue words that signal a cause: *as a result, because, since.*

Use information from this page to complete the chart below.

WRITE HERE

Why? Cause	What Happened? Effect
Since the mountains in some parts of Asia are very steep,	_____
_____	As a result, in Africa and Australia, many people still use camels.

Travelers in Nepal use a tuin to cross a large river.

rural (RUR-uhl) to do with the countryside or farming. Rural areas have few people living there.

Find Effects for a Cause

The **effect** is the result of what happened. Sometimes, one cause may have many effects. Read about rope bridges and complete the chart below. The chart is started for you.

Over the River

Think about your environment. What is the land like? Do you have to cross rivers? Do you pass over steep mountains? Is the land flat? Is it wet?

Throughout time, people have adapted to their environments. A river, for example, can block travelers. People built bridges to connect pieces of land.

The first bridge might have been a log or rock placed over a stream. But imagine trying to get from place to place in the steep mountains. In some parts of the world, many people in **rural** areas still use rope bridges. These bridges hang across a valley or river.

These bridges are made from rope and wood. Because there are no cars in the area, the bridges are narrow. Only people and animals use them, not cars. Some bridges hang hundreds of feet above rivers!

WRITE HERE

Cause: Because there are no cars in the area,

Effect: *bridges are narrow*

Effect: _____

_____

© 2003 Options Publishing Inc.

In Asia, there is a small country called Nepal. Many people in Nepal use a bridge called a *tuin* (TOO-in). A huge wire connects to both sides of the river. A wooden basket hangs from the wire. The traveler pulls the basket along the wire.

In many big cities, thousands of cars, buses, and trucks cross bridges every day. In some cities in the United States, there are huge bridges: the Golden Gate Bridge in San Francisco, California, and the Brooklyn Bridge in New York City. Some bridges are small. Others are large. People use the environment to meet their needs.

The Brooklyn Bridge carries thousands of people to and from Brooklyn, New York.

Use Cause and Effect to Draw a Conclusion

When you **draw a conclusion**, you make a statement that sums up the meaning of the information you read. To help draw a conclusion, look for the cause of an event. Then look for what happens as a result.

WRITE HERE

The author says that in some cities in the United States there are huge bridges. List one reason why these cities need such big bridges. Hint: Look for a cause.

_____

_____

_____

_____

© 2003 Options Publishing Inc.

protect (pruh-TEKT) to guard or keep something safe from harm, attack, or injury.

Homes

For thousands of years, people have used things from nature to build their homes. People need to **protect** themselves from the weather. That's why a home in the hot, dry desert looks very different from a home in the cold Arctic.

Many Inuit live in northern Canada. This environment is very cold. Today, most of the people live in wooden houses. Years ago, the people built homes called igloos. The walls and dome-shaped roofs were made of thick blocks of snow. The roof and walls kept the people safe from the wind and cold. People also used sealskins to cover the doorway. Sealskins also made warm bed covers.

Snowshoes stand ready for use outside an igloo in Canada.

WRITE HERE

The author tells you that people have used things from nature to build their homes. Read about the Inuit. List two examples of what they used from nature to build their homes.

1. _____

2. _____

Traditional houses in Indonesia have high, sloping roofs to protect people from the sun. The roofs also allow heavy rains to drain away.

Find Cause and Effect

When authors use **causes** and **effects**, they do not always give you clue words, such as *because* or *as a result*. You must put why something happens together with what happens as a result. Complete the chart below about how people build houses depending on their type of weather.

In tropical places in the world, houses are very different. Indonesia, for example, is very hot. At certain times of the year, heavy rains fall. The people make their homes from bamboo. Traditional houses have sloping roofs made of leaves and grasses. The roof protects people from the sun. It also helps drain rainwater away from the house. The sides are open so that the breeze blows through the house. This helps keep the house cool.

Deserts are hot and dry. Many homes have flat roofs. People don't need to worry about rain or snow on the roofs. The walls are very thick. The windows are small. Thick walls protect people from the heat and the sun. Inside the houses, the temperature is much cooler than outside.

WRITE HERE

Cause	Effect
1. In Indonesia, the weather is very hot and wet.	_____ _____
2. Deserts are hot and dry.	_____ _____

Figure Out Cause and Effect

The **cause** makes the **effect** happen. Which is the cause in these sentences? People in cold climates cannot grow lemons. Lemons do not grow in cold areas. Add a signal word: *Since* lemon trees do not grow in cold areas (cause), people in cold climates cannot grow lemon trees (effect).

What's for Dinner?

Where people live also helps them decide what they will grow. Today, trucks and planes bring people foods from all parts of the world. But even a century ago, people ate food that was grown only in their area.

People living in very cold, snowy areas could not plant lemon or orange trees. These trees need warm weather to grow.

A worker sorts oranges before they go to market.

People living on islands or near rivers ate fish. The Inuit ate fish, seals, and whales. People living in warm areas grew fruit.

Because environments around the world are different, the foods people plant and eat are also different.

In many parts of Asia, spring and summer are hot and humid. There is heavy rainfall. In this part of the world, rice grows well. Rice is a main part of many Asian diets.

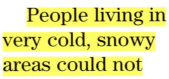
WRITE HERE

Underline the cause and circle the effect.

1. Because some parts of Asia have hot weather with a lot of rainfall, rice grows very well there.

2. Rice is an important part of many Asian diets, because parts of Asia grow a lot of rice.

3. Since trucks and planes deliver food from all over the world, many people can eat foods that are grown in other areas.

Rice needs a wet environment. Millet is a grass-like wheat grown for its small seeds. Millet needs little water. It grows well in drier areas. Millet grows in parts of India and Africa. It is a main part of the people's diet there.

In Central and South America, crops like bananas, coffee, and cocoa grow well. These crops need high temperatures. They also need heavy rainfall to grow. The average temperature in Central America is 86°F. It gets about 209 inches of rain per year. This environment is perfect for these crops.

Our environment shapes how we live. It shapes how we travel and the types of houses we build. People have learned to use what is around them. How does your environment shape the way you live? ■

NET CONNECTION
http://www.ibiblio.org/sashley/homes

Understand Cause and Effect

You learned that the **cause** makes the **effect** happen. Authors do not always give you signal words, such as *because*, *since*, or *as a result*, to show cause and effect. Turn the sentences below into cause-and-effect statements by adding the correct signal words.

WRITE HERE

as a result   **because**

Add one of the signal words above to each sentence to make it a cause-and-effect statement.

1. _____ millet needs little water, it grows well in dry areas.

2. Central America has warm temperatures and a lot of rainfall, and _____ , bananas, coffee, and cocoa grow very well.

Understand a Photograph

A **primary source** is a document or piece of artwork that people make about something they do or an event they see happen. Photographs, diaries and journals written at the time, and some artwork are examples of primary sources.

A **community** is a group of people who live in the same area or who share the same interests. Study the photograph of a community in Hong Kong. Then answer the questions.

Boats, called junks, are homes for some people in Hong Kong.

WRITE HERE

1. List two reasons why the river is important to this community.

   a. _____

   b. _____

2. List one type of transportation used by the people in this community.

   _____

3. What food do you think is important to this community? Why?

   _____

Compare and Contrast Using a Venn Diagram

When you **compare**, you tell how people, places, and things are alike. When you **contrast**, you tell how they are different. Comparing and contrasting helps you understand information in a picture or an article.

Use the photograph on page 14 and the following questions to complete the **Venn diagram** below:

1. List one way your community is different from the Hong Kong community.

2. List one way the Hong Kong community is different from your community.

3. List one way that both your community and the Hong Kong community are alike.

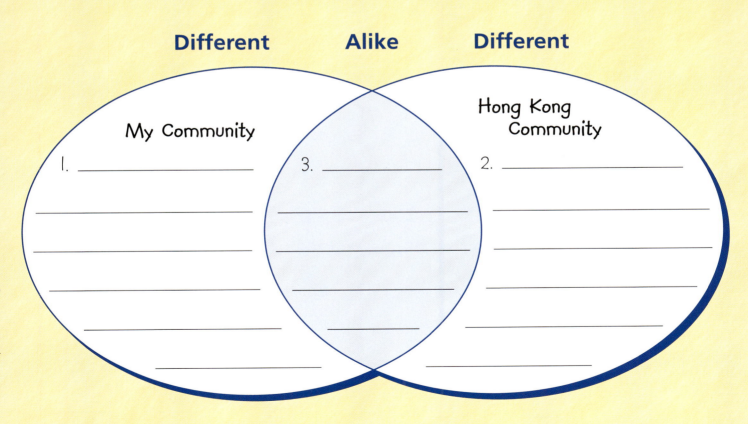

Different   **Alike**   **Different**

My Community

1. _____

Hong Kong Community

3. _____

2. _____

Use Cause and Effect to Write a Postcard

Think about your community. What kinds of foods are grown in your area? What are your houses like? How do you travel? Think about *why* your environment shapes what you do.

Write a **postcard** to someone who lives in a completely different type of community. First, complete the chart. Then use the information to help you write a postcard describing the environment in your community.

Travel	
Homes	
Food Grown	

Using Maps

Maps help you find out about places. To understand maps, you need to know what the symbols mean. You also need to read the titles and figure out what the shapes and colors mean. A map forms a picture that tells about the location of a place.

Think About Maps

A **map** is a flat drawing that shows you what real places look like from above. For example, stand up and look down at the top of your desk. This could be a map of your desktop. Now imagine it is the world. This is the view that maps look at. Maps use colors, lines, and shapes to show information about different parts of the world. In this lesson, you will learn about different kinds of maps.

To read a map, follow these steps:

• Look at the **map title**. It tells you what the map shows.

• Look at the **map key**, or **legend**. It tells you what the symbols and features on the map stand for. Symbols are objects that stand for something else.

• Look for the **compass rose**. This shows you directions on the map.

• Look to see if there is a **map scale**. The scale shows distances on a map. It can be a line marked in miles, kilometers, or both.

Think About the Topic

Read **Think About Maps**. Then write the correct label from the box next to each picture. When you have finished this map lesson, check to see if your answers are correct.

compass rose	map key

★ State capital _____
● City
— State border _____

_____

Using Maps
Physical Map/Landforms

Question

Read the title of the map on this page. Ask yourself: *What is this map about? What does it show?* A **physical map** shows major natural features, such as mountains or rivers, on the earth's surface. These are called **landforms**. A **plain** is a large, flat lowland.

WRITE HERE

Below are four landforms from the map. Write the landform next to the correct definition. Use the map to help you.

mountain   plain   island   lake

_____ a body of land surrounded by water on all sides

_____ a large body of water with land all around it

_____ sloping land that rises high above the land around it

_____ a large, flat lowland

Physical Map: Read Symbols

This **physical map** of the United States shows landforms. It uses symbols to show mountains and rivers. A **symbol** is an object that stands for something else. Look at the map key. The symbol for a mountain is ⌗. The symbol for a river is ⌐.

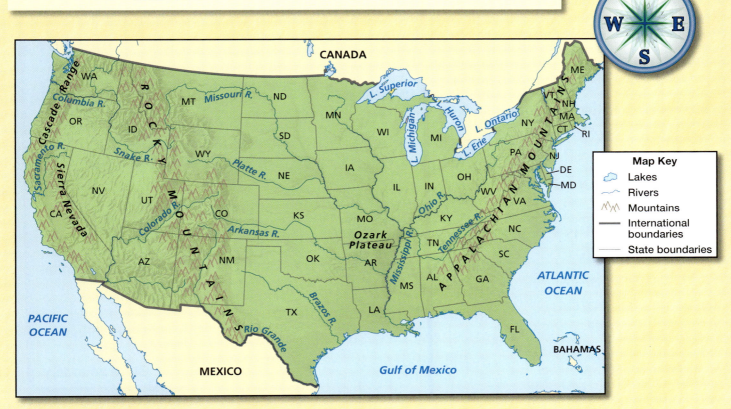

Map Key
- Lakes
- Rivers
- Mountains
- International boundaries
- State boundaries

WRITE HERE

1. Write the state where you can find the mountains called the Sierra Nevada.

2. Are the Appalachian Mountains closer to the East Coast or the West Coast of the United States?

3. Which major river runs through Nebraska (NE)?

4. Name the mountain range that runs through Utah (UT).

Read a Compass Rose

A **compass rose** tells you the directions on a map. There are four places: north, east, south, and west. These four places are called **cardinal** directions. By using the compass rose, you can see that Wisconsin (WI) is north of Illinois (IL). You can also see that California (CA) is west of Virginia (VA).

Political Maps

A **political map** shows how people have divided up the earth's surface. The political map on the next page shows how the United States is divided into states.

The map also has a **map key**. This key uses symbols to show the national capital of the United States.

You'll also find symbols for state capitals and large cities. A thin line shows you the boundaries, or borders, between the states. The thick line shows you where the national boundaries are. These boundaries show where the United States end and other countries begin.

Read the map title. This tells you what the map is about.

Different maps give different information. Sometimes you have to use more than one map to get all the information you want. This map, for example, does not show two states: Alaska and Hawaii.

Symbols

Map Key
- ⊛ National capital
- ★ State capital
- • City
- ─── International boundary
- ─── State boundary

WRITE HERE

1. List the three bodies of water that surround the United States.

   a. _____

   b. _____

   c. _____

2. If you were in Austin, Texas, in which direction would you go to get to Tallahassee, Florida?

   _____

Political Map: The United States of America

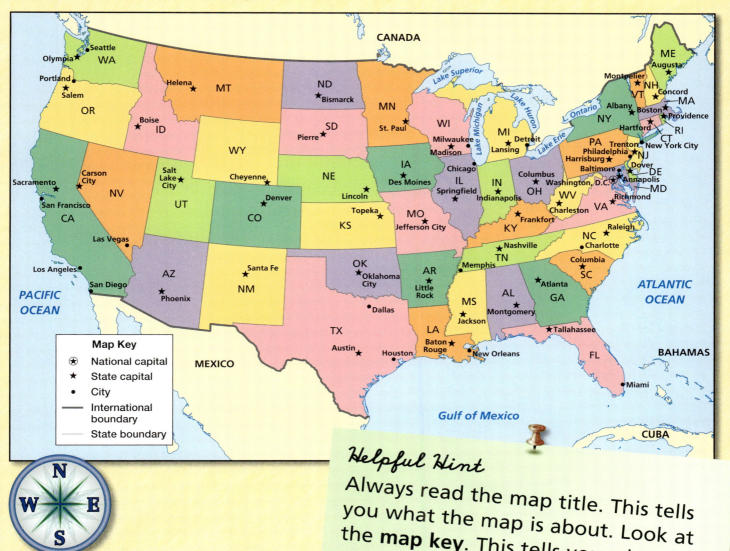

Map Key
- ⍟ National capital
- ★ State capital
- • City
- ▬ International boundary
- — State boundary

Helpful Hint
Always read the map title. This tells you what the map is about. Look at the **map key**. This tells you what the symbols stand for.

WRITE HERE

3. What is the symbol used to show a state capital?

_____

4. Find the state you live in. What is your state's capital?

_____

5. List the two countries that border the United States.

a. _____

b. _____

Understand a Globe

Imagine that you are an astronaut. You look out the window of your spacecraft toward Earth. What you see looks like a blue marble. You notice that there are white swirls over the surface. These are clouds.

To have a better understanding of Earth, people have made globes. A **globe** is a model of Earth. It is a ball, or sphere, with a map wrapped around it. To look at a globe in a book, the globe is cut in half.

On the globe, there are imaginary lines. These lines tell people where different places on Earth are. The **equator** is the line around the middle of Earth. At the equator, Earth can be divided into two parts. Each part is a hemisphere. Hemi means "half." The half of Earth above the equator is the Northern Hemisphere. The half below the equator is the Southern Hemisphere.

Another imaginary line is the **prime meridian**. It divides Earth into the Eastern Hemisphere and the Western Hemisphere.

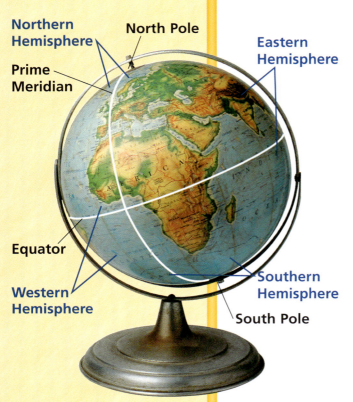

Northern Hemisphere

North Pole

Eastern Hemisphere

Prime Meridian

Equator

Western Hemisphere

Southern Hemisphere

South Pole

WRITE HERE

1. Does the equator run from the top to the bottom of the globe or through the middle of the globe?

_____

2. The prime meridian divides the globe into the Western Hemisphere and the _____ Hemisphere.

3. Is the Southern Hemisphere at the top or the bottom of the globe?

Read a Hemisphere Map

Here are two maps showing Earth flattened out. They show you the Western Hemisphere and the Eastern Hemisphere. The top half of the globe above the equator is the Northern Hemisphere. The bottom half of the globe below the equator is the Southern Hemisphere. These maps also show the seven continents and the four oceans.

Map of the Hemispheres

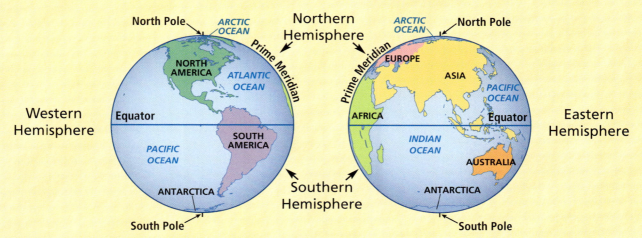

WRITE HERE

Study the maps above and answer the questions.

1. List the seven continents.

a. _____   e. _____

b. _____   f. _____

c. _____   g. _____

d. _____

2. List the four oceans.

a. _____   c. _____

b. _____   d. _____

Special Purpose: Distribution Map

Some maps are called **special purpose maps**. They often show climates or populations.

One kind of special purpose map is called a **distribution (dis-tri-BYOO-shuhn) map**. It shows how things are spread out across an area. Some distribution maps show where corn is grown throughout the world. Others might show where all the schools are in your city.

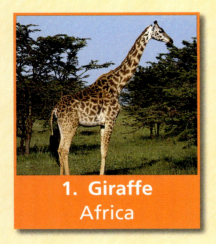

1. Giraffe
Africa

2. Panda
Asia

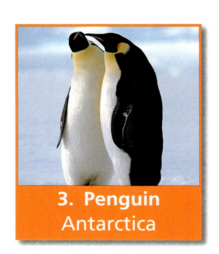

3. Penguin
Antarctica

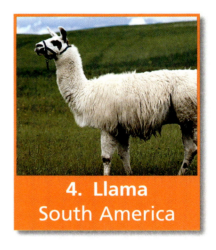

4. Llama
South America

WRITE HERE

This map shows the seven continents. Around the map are pictures of animals. Some of these animals can now be found in many places around the world. But these animals are native to the continents listed under their pictures.

1. In each blank box on the map, write in the number for the animal that belongs on each continent.

Wild Animals of the World

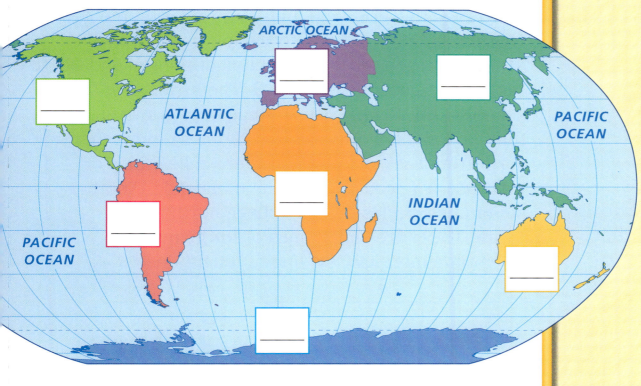

ARCTIC OCEAN

ATLANTIC OCEAN

PACIFIC OCEAN

PACIFIC OCEAN

INDIAN OCEAN

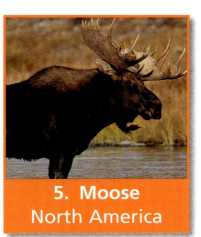

5. Moose
North America

6. Wild Boar
Europe

7. Kangaroo
Australia

WRITE HERE

2. What does this distribution map show?

_____

3. Write the name of the continent on which you live.

_____

Read a Grid Map

A **grid map** is made from two sets of lines that cross. One set of lines goes east to west. The other set goes north to south. These lines are called a grid system. They help you locate places on a map. Study the map and answer the questions below.

Community Grid Map

To read this grid map, put your finger on the **Grammar School**. Look to the left or right of the school. You see the letter **B**. Look at the top and the bottom. You see the number **3**. The location of the school is **B3**. People use an imaginary grid system that covers the world. One set of lines circles the earth from east to west. These are called lines of **latitude**. The equator is a line of latitude. Another set of lines circles the earth from north to south. These are called lines of **longitude**. The prime meridian is a line of longitude.

	1	2	3	4	5	
A	Post Office				Park	A
B			Grammar School		Police Station	B
C	Community Center					C
D					Fire Station	D
	1	2	3	4	5	

WRITE HERE

Write the location of the grid square for each place listed:

1. Community Center _____
2. Police Station _____
3. Park _____
4. Post Office _____
5. Fire Station _____
6. Grammar School _____

Read a Climate Map

Another type of special purpose map is a **climate map**. **Climate** is the kind of weather a place has from year to year. This climate map shows the average weather conditions in two continents: North America and South America. Study the map and answer the questions below.

The Climate in North America and South America

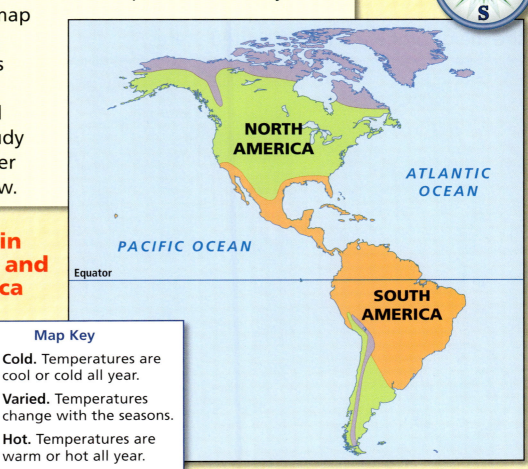

Map Key

Cold. Temperatures are cool or cold all year.

Varied. Temperatures change with the seasons.

Hot. Temperatures are warm or hot all year.

WRITE HERE

1. List the three types of climates in South America.

a. _____   c. _____

b. _____

2. Compare the green area with the orange area. How does the climate affect the way people live, what they wear, and what vegetables or fruits they grow?

_____

_____

Read a Road Map

NET CONNECTION
Draw your own maps at
http://www.smartdraw.com

When you want to plan a trip to a new place, a
road map helps. It shows all the roads in a certain
area. The road map on this page shows some of
the major highways in the United States.

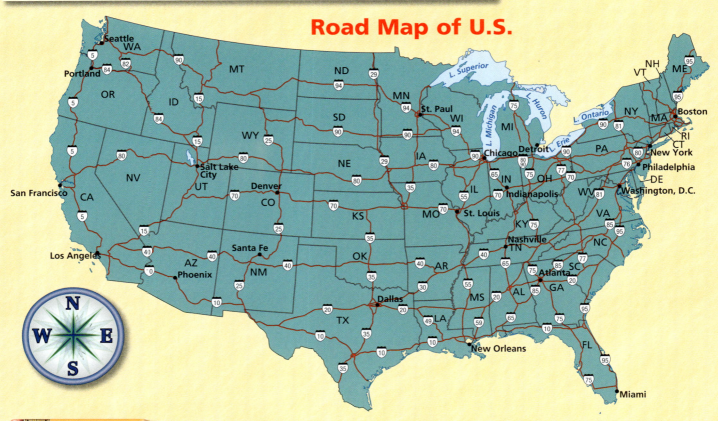

Road Map of U.S.

WRITE HERE

Study the map and answer the questions.

1. If you wanted to travel from San Francisco, California (CA),
   to Salt Lake City, Utah (UT),

   a. in which direction would
   you travel?

   b. which highway would get
   you there the fastest?

   _____

2. Which highway goes from Arizona (AZ) all the way to
   Arkansas (AR)?

   _____

The First Communities

People have not always lived in cities. People used to live by hunting animals and gathering wild fruits and nuts. Then, about 10,000 years ago, people learned to raise animals and grow crops. For the first time, people settled in one place. Communities formed when people worked and lived together.

Think About Drawing Conclusions

When you **draw a conclusion**, you make a decision about the meaning of information, facts and details, in what you read. Often, authors want you to draw a conclusion from what you read. You must use your own ideas along with facts and details in your reading.

To draw conclusions, follow these tips:

- Look for the facts and details. Facts and details are the pieces of information in a story.

- Use what you already know about what you are reading.

- Make a statement that sums up the meaning of the information you read.

People learned to raise animals and grow crops.

+

People settled in one place.

=

Conclusion

Communities formed when people worked and lived together.

Think About the Topic

Reread the paragraph at the top of the page. Then quickly look through the article. Look at the headings, pictures, and maps on pages 29–40. What do you think this article is about?

_____

_____

gatherer
(gaTH-ur-ur)
a person who finds and collects food in the wild.

Question

Headings in an article help you predict the main idea. Change each heading into a question. As you read, try to answer these questions.

Early hunters drew pictures on cave walls.

The First Communities

Hunters and Gatherers

Long ago, people did not have a home in one place. Instead, they traveled to find food. They did not know how to farm. They did not buy food in stores. There were no stores. Early people are called hunters and **gatherers** because that is how they got their food.

Hunters followed moving herds of animals, such as deer and bison. Usually, men did the hunting.

Early people also gathered, or collected, wild fruits, seeds, and berries. People had to learn which plants were safe to eat. Depending on the weather, hunters and gatherers could only find certain foods just a short time each year. Often, women gathered the food from plants.

Hunters and gatherers were always on the move. They were looking for food. Communities began when people settled in one place and began to farm.

WRITE HERE

When you change the heading **Hunters and Gatherers** into a question, you ask: *Who are hunters and gatherers?* Read this section and answer the question.

Hunters and gatherers are

_____

_____

_____

© 2003 Options Publishing Inc.

Making a Civilization

About 10,000 years ago, communities grew into towns and then cities. These early communities became civilizations. But what is a civilization?

==Civilizations are different from hunter and gatherer **societies**.==

- They have a government.
- They have buildings that are meant to last a long time.
- They have a way to grow food.
- They have people who do different jobs.
- They may have a system of writing.

Civilizations have laws. The people try to work together.

A mosaic is a picture made up of small pieces of tile. This mosaic is from 14th century Venice, Italy. It shows workers building a tower.

society all the people who live in the same country or area and share the same laws and customs.

Understand Conclusions

Support your **conclusion** with facts and details. The author draws a conclusion: Civilizations are different from hunter and gatherer societies. As you read, look for facts and details that support this conclusion.

WRITE HERE

List two facts from this page that support the author's conclusion.

1. Fact:

_____

2. Fact:

_____

© 2003 Options Publishing Inc.

crescent
(KRESS-uhnt) a curved shape that looks like the moon when it is a sliver in the sky.

fertile (FUR-tuhl) good for growing crops; rich.

Support a Conclusion

When you **draw a conclusion**, check the facts and details. Make sure they support your conclusion. Read this page about the Fertile Crescent. Then answer the question below.

The Fertile Crescent

One of the first civilizations began in a place called the **Fertile Crescent**. The eastern part of the Fertile Crescent comes between two rivers. This area is called Mesopotamia (mes-suh-puh-TAH-mee-ah). Today, the country of Iraq is here. The name Mesopotamia means "land between the rivers." The rivers are the Tigris (TEYE-gruhs) and Euphrates (you-FRAY-teez).

Because of these rivers, people had rich soil to grow crops. When a river floods, soil is left on the riverbanks. Land along the banks of a river is often fertile. It is good for growing crops. Farmers also use rivers to water their crops. People began to settle in one place. They built homes and farmed the land.

Villagers look down at the Euphrates River in eastern Syria.

WRITE HERE

Rivers were important to forming a civilization in the Fertile Crescent. List two ways that rivers helped form a civilization.

1. _____

2. _____

The Fertile Crescent and Important Cities

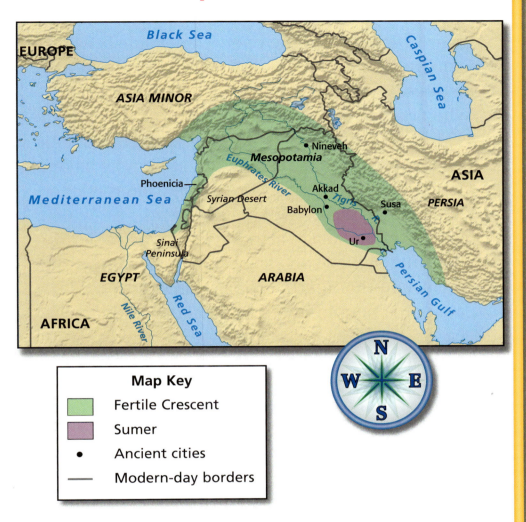

Map Key

🟩	Fertile Crescent
🟪	Sumer
•	Ancient cities
—	Modern-day borders

Draw a Conclusion from a Map

A **map** is a flat drawing. It shows you what a place looks like from above. You have read about the Tigris and Euphrates rivers. Locate the rivers on the map. You can see what the whole area looks like. Study the map and answer the questions below.

WRITE HERE

1. Find the city of Babylon on the map. Think about if you were to travel from Babylon to Ur. Would you travel over the land or sail on the river?

2. Explain your answer.

Communities Form in Mesopotamia

People need water, food, and a place to live. The Sumerians (soo-MER-ee-ans) lived in Mesopotamia. They used water from the river. They made bread from wheat. They grew grapes. Food and oil came from olive trees. People burned the oil in lamps for light.

When people began to farm, they no longer had to travel to find food. This meant they could build homes. These homes were often made of mud bricks baked in the hot sun. Some homes were made from reeds. Reeds are tall grasses with hollow stems.

Settling in one place also meant it was easier to keep farm animals, such as sheep, goats, and cattle. Farmers sold their extra crops. This is how trade began. Some people traded pots, tools, and jewelry for food.

Over time, people built roads to connect one place to another. The Sumerians used sailboats on the Tigris and Euphrates rivers. The roads and rivers allowed trade to spread to new places.

Sumerians made clay pots to hold food, water, or oil.

Find Facts to Draw a Conclusion

Read "Communities Form in Mesopotamia." Think about the conclusions you can draw. Then answer the question.

WRITE HERE

Farming helped early people form a community.

Do you agree with this conclusion? Use details from the article to explain your answer.

_____

_____

People Learn to Write

The Sumerians were the first people to begin to write. They wrote down many of their stories and their history. They were also the first people to tell time by dividing up an hour and separating it into 60 minutes.

A Government Forms

Small villages along the rivers began to grow into larger cities. As cities grew, they became more powerful. The generals from these cities became powerful. Later on, they were made kings.

Nearly 4000 years ago, a king named Hammurabi (ha-muh-RAH-bee) fought the Sumerians and others living in the Fertile Crescent. He won and became their king. He wrote a set of laws for the people. A government was born.

Jobs

People in these cities were not all farmers or soldiers. Many found other jobs and traded their skills for food. Different people in the community did different jobs. Some people learned to make bronze from copper and tin. They made strong tools with this new metal.

Draw Conclusions Using Context Clues

Often, an author tells you the meaning of a new word by giving you a **synonym clue**. A **synonym** is a word that means the same or almost the same as another word. *Happy* and *cheerful* are synonyms.

WRITE HERE

Read this sentence from the article. Write the synonym clue that the author uses to help you understand what the word *divide* means.

They also were the first people to tell time by *dividing* up an hour and separating it into 60 minutes.

_____

The Great Sailors

The Phoenicians (fi-NEE-shuns) lived in the western part of the Fertile Crescent. This area is near the Mediterranean Sea. There is no country of Phoenicia today. Today, the countries of Israel, Lebanon, and Syria are here.

The Phoenicians were known for their skill as sailors. The Phoenicians traveled by sea to trade. They sold beautiful glass and purple cloth. They bought silver, copper, and tin. They built cities in faraway places to make trading easier.

One of the most important things the Phoenicians did was to create an alphabet. It had 22 letters and no vowels. This alphabet changed over time and became the one we use today.

Draw Your Own Conclusion

When you **draw a conclusion**, always look for facts and details that support the conclusion.

Were the Phoenicians really a civilization? Draw a conclusion. Write it below.

The Phoenician alphabet had 22 letters. The Greeks added vowels. Later, the Romans changed the alphabet for writing Latin.

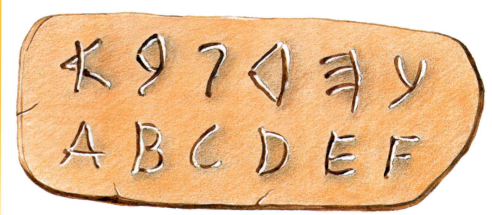

WRITE HERE

My Conclusion:

_____

_____

_____

Write two facts that support your conclusion.

1. _____

_____

2. _____

_____

Life on the Nile

Another important civilization lived along the Nile River in Egypt. Without the Nile, Egypt would have been too dry for farming or living in communities.

The Nile is the longest river in the world. The Nile flooded its banks every year. (Today, dams keep it in place.) As in Mesopotamia, this flooding helped the farmers. The Egyptians grew wheat and barley in the rich soil. They grew a plant called flax. By weaving the fibers of this plant into thread, they made cloth.

The Egyptians sailed the Nile to trade goods with others. They used pictures and symbols called hieroglyphics (hye-ruh-GLIF-iks) as their writing. They were ruled by kings called pharaohs (FAIR-ohz).

We continue to learn from these ancient civilizations. People began as hunters and gatherers. Then, they built communities. These communities grew into great civilizations. ■

Egyptians used pictures and symbols called hieroglyphics as their writing.

NET CONNECTION
http://carlos.emory.edu/ODYSSEY

Draw Conclusions by Comparing

Comparing how two things are alike can help you draw conclusions. Remember, your conclusion must still be supported by facts and details.

Read this page. Think of the other civilizations you read about. Think about what conclusions you can draw. Then answer the questions.

WRITE HERE

1. In what way was Egypt like another civilization described in this article?

_____

_____

2. Think about where these early communities began. What did all the communities you read about have in common?

_____

_____

Draw Conclusions from What You See

This **photograph** shows reed houses on the banks of the Tigris River in southern Iraq. Before 1991, these houses were made by the Marsh Arabs, who gathered the reeds that grew around the rivers. Experts think that these houses looked the same as those built by the Sumerians thousands of years ago! Study the photograph and answer the questions below.

WRITE HERE

1. List three details that tell you what the photo is about.

a. _____

b. _____

c. _____

2. Look at the people. Think about the weather. What do you already know about what you see in the photo?

_____

_____

3. Why do you think people still make their houses from reeds?

_____

_____

Draw Conclusions by Comparing and Contrasting

A **Venn diagram** is a good tool to use when you compare and contrast information. In the middle, where the two circles overlap, write the ways your community and ancient communities are alike. Write the things that are different in your community on the left. Then write the things that are different in ancient communities on the right.

Before you write, work in a small group. Think about how these things are the same or different: government, houses, food, and jobs. Look back at the article if you need more details. The diagram is started for you.

Different　　　**Alike**　　　**Different**

My Community

• don't live near a river

_____

_____

_____

_____

_____

built homes

• built homes

_____

_____

_____

Ancient Communities

• lived near a river

_____

_____

_____

_____

Draw Conclusions in an Opinion

Think about the community you live in today. Is it like the ancient communities you read about in this article? Or is it very different than the ancient communities? Write your opinion, what you think, in a complete sentence. Then support your opinion by explaining why you think this way. Be sure to include facts and details that support your opinion. Use the Venn diagram you completed on page 39 to help you.

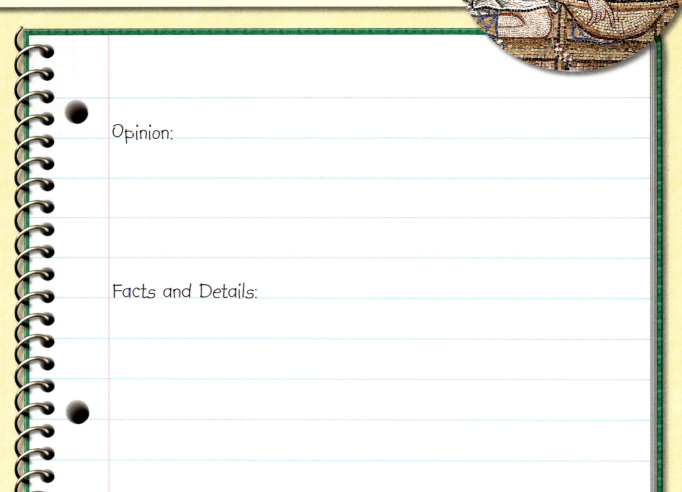

Opinion:

Facts and Details:

Using Graphs and Charts

Graphs and charts arrange information so that it is easy to read and to understand. It is important to know how to read graphs and charts. These skills help you understand information.

Think About Graphs and Charts

Graphs and **charts** arrange facts and information. They show facts in a picture. Did you know that China has 227 million homes with TVs? The United States has 97 million. Russia has 48 million homes with TVs. Japan has 41 million. When you read these numbers, it is hard to see how they compare with one another. Now look at the same information in a bar graph.

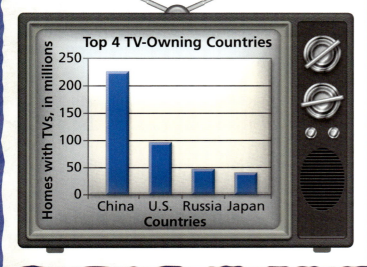

You can quickly see the difference between the countries by looking at the height of the bars. To read a graph, follow these steps:

- Look at the whole graph and read the **title**. This tells what the graph is about.

- Read the **labels**: "Homes with TVs" and "Countries." These tell how the information is arranged.

Think About the Topic

Use the information in **Think About Graphs and Charts** to answer this question:

What other type of information could best be shown in a graph or a chart? List two examples.

1. _____

2. _____

Understand Bar Graphs

A **bar graph** helps you compare things. In this bar graph, the continents are compared. The numbers on the left tell the number of inches of precipitation (pri-sip-I-TAY-shuhn) per year. Precipitation is water from the sky in the form of rain, sleet, hail, or snow.

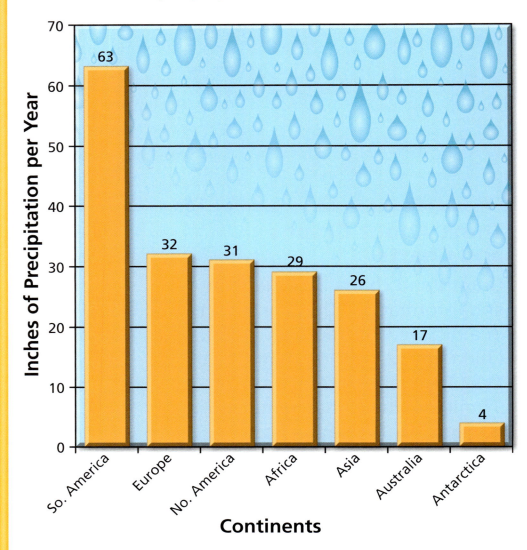

Inches of Precipitation per Year for the Seven Continents

WRITE HERE

Study the bar graph and answer these questions.

1. What is being compared in this bar graph?

_____

2. Which continent gets the most precipitation in a year?

_____

3. How much more precipitation does South America get than Europe gets? Show your work.

_____

Make Your Own Bar Graph

Bar graphs use numbers and bars to compare two or more things. Read the information in the next paragraph. Then turn the information into a bar graph.

Your school is raising money for the Community Food Bank. Your class sells 20 apples, 5 pencils, 10 tee shirts, and 15 pens.

Turn the information into a bar graph. Be sure to give your graph a title and add labels.

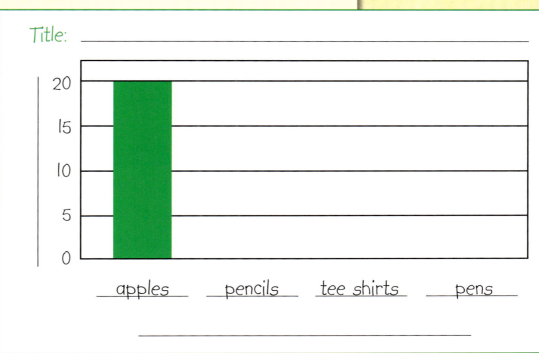

Title: _____

apples   pencils   tee shirts   pens

_____

WRITE HERE

Use your bar graph to answer these questions.

1. How many more pens than pencils did your class sell? Show your work.

_____

2. How many items did your class sell all together?

_____

3. Your class sold tee shirts for $3.00 each. How much money did the class make by selling tee shirts?

_____

Understand Line Graphs

Line graphs show how something changes over time. Read the **title** and **labels**. They tell you what the graph is about. In this graph, the side label tells you the number of people in the United States in millions. The label at the bottom tells you the years in which the people were counted.

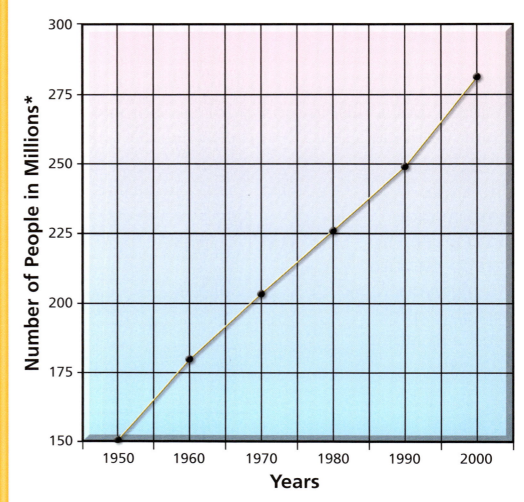

The Growing Population of the United States 1950–2000

*Population is rounded off to the nearest million.

WRITE HERE

1. What is this line graph about?

_____

2. Circle the letter of the sentence that is the best conclusion for this line graph.

   A. The number of people in the United States is decreasing.

   B. The number of people in the United States is increasing.

3. Think about what the graph shows you about the population of the United States from 1950 to 2000. Use the graph to draw a conclusion. Do you think there will be more people in 2020 or fewer people? Why?

_____

_____

 # Understand Tables

Tables, or charts, organize facts into a small space. You can find tables and charts in your social studies, math, reading, and science books.

Imagine that you are taking a trip to London, England. Look at the table. It shows you the average temperature for each month in London, England.

To quickly see how the temperature changes, turn the table into a line graph. The graph is started for you.

Average Monthly Temperatures, London, England			
Month	Temperature °F	Month	Temperature °F
January	41	July	72
February	44	August	72
March	50	September	64
April	55	October	57
May	63	November	48
June	68	December	45

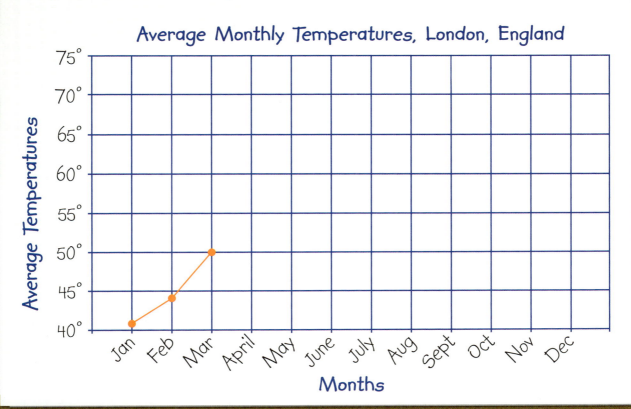

Average Monthly Temperatures, London, England

Understand Diagrams

A **diagram** is a drawing that shows the parts of something. Diagrams help explain how things go together or how they work. The title tells what the diagram is about. Some diagrams also include a **key** that shows what the words or symbols in the drawing mean. Read the information about ants. Study the diagram. Then answer the questions on page 47.

Amazing Ants

Did you know that about 9,500 different kinds of ants have been discovered? Scientists guess that there are about 20,000 different kinds in all. Ants have been living on the earth for about 100 million years. They are social insects. They live in large communities called colonies.

Diagram of the Head of an Ant

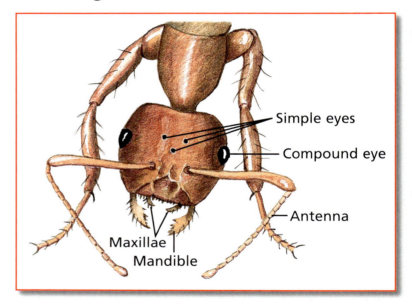

Word Key

Antennae (an-TEN-ee)   These feelers allow the ant to touch, taste, smell, and feel movement.

Compound eyes   All ants have two compound eyes. They look like cut jewels. People have one lens in each eye. Ants have many lenses. Each lens sees a small part of what the ant is looking at. Together, the lenses form a whole picture. These eyes let the ant see movement easily.

Simple eyes   Male and queen ants also have three simple eyes. These eyes help the ants see any changes in the amount of light.

Mandibles (MAN-duh-buhls)   These are a pair of jaws. They move from side to side. Ants use them for fighting, digging, and carrying objects.

Maxillae (mak-SI-lee)   These are found behind the mandibles. They are used for chewing food. They also have rows of little hairs. The ant uses these to clean its legs and antennae.

WRITE HERE

Study the diagram and answer the questions.

1. What is the title of the diagram?

_____

2. How many parts are there to an ant's head?

_____

3. List the ways an ant uses its mandibles.

a. _____

b. _____

c. _____

4. How does the Word Key help you understand the diagram?

_____

_____

5. Why do you think it is important for ants to clean their antennae?

_____

_____

_____

Understand Flowcharts

A **flowchart** shows you the correct steps in a process. It is made of pictures, words, or boxes. Flowcharts use arrows or numbers to show which step comes next. Look at the pictures. Follow the numbers. They tell you the correct order of the steps. This flowchart shows you how to make an origami hat. Origami (or-uh-GAH-mee) is the Japanese art of paper folding. Have an adult help you.

Making an Origami Hat

1. Start with a large piece of newspaper. Cut it so that it makes a square. Fold the corner down, point to point.

2. Turn paper with point down. Fold left and right corners to bottom point.

3. Fold the two flaps up.

4. Now fold the two flaps down. Then fold the two points out.

5. Look at the bottom point. Take just the upper flap and fold it up.

6. This is what your hat looks like so far.

7. Fold the upper flap up.

8. Fold the bottom flap behind.

This is what your hat looks like.

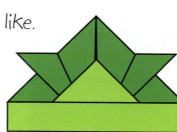

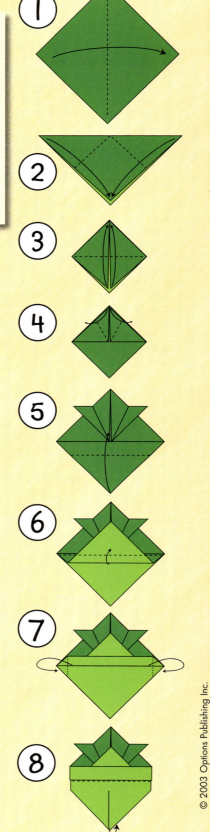

WRITE HERE

Study the flowchart and answer the questions.

Circle the letter of the answer that best completes the questions.

1. This flowchart is about

   A. studying the Japanese culture.

   B. making an origami hat.

   C. folding newspaper.

   D. learning about ancient Japan.

2. How many steps are shown in the flowchart?

   A. 6

   B. 14

   C. 8

   D. 5

3. A flowchart is used to show

   A. how things are alike or different.

   B. the difference between facts and opinions.

   C. how things change over time.

   D. the steps in a process.

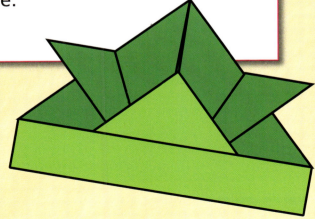

Understand Circle Graphs

A **circle graph** shows you the parts of a whole. It divides the whole into parts, called sectors. Circle graphs are also called pie graphs because the graph looks like a pie. Each sector, or slice of pie, is written as a percentage. These numbers in the circle graph add up to 100%. Remember that *whole* means 100%.

In this circle graph, each type of vehicle is shown in a different color.

Study the circle graph and answer the questions.

1. Are there more trucks or cars/taxis on the highways?

_____

2. What is the difference in the percentage between trucks and cars/taxis? Show your work.

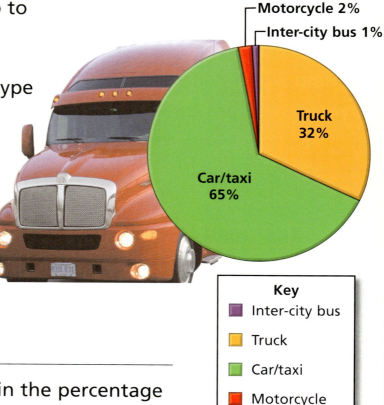

Who Uses American Highways?

Motorcycle 2%
Inter-city bus 1%
Truck 32%
Car/taxi 65%

Key

- ■ Inter-city bus
- ■ Truck
- ■ Car/taxi
- ■ Motorcycle

Make Your Own Circle Graph

Graphs help you see information easily. Read the paragraph below about the kinds of pets people have.

Juan and Anita want to find out what kinds of pets people in their class own. They took a survey by asking their classmates which animals they had at home. There are 20 students in the class. Ten people (50%) owned dogs. Five people (25%) owned cats. Two people (10%) owned goldfish. Three people (15%) owned hamsters.

Help Juan and Anita easily understand this information. Make a **circle graph**. The circle graph has been started for you. Notice that there are two light lines dividing the graph into quarters, or sections that equal 25%. This will help you guess how to divide the circle into the correct sectors, or slices.

Title: _Class Pets_

Goldfish 10%

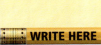
WRITE HERE

Answer these questions about your circle graph.

1. What is the total percentage of all the sectors, or slices? Show your work.

2. Which type of pet do most people own?

_____

3. Write your own question based on the graph you just made.

_____

_____

Understand Time Lines

A **time line** is a type of flowchart. It shows events in the order in which they happened. This type of graph helps you understand and remember when events happened. A time line also shows how much time passes between events.

Always read the title of the time line. This time line gives you a history of classic American toy inventions. Read the dates at the beginning and end of the time line. These dates tell the period of time that is covered.

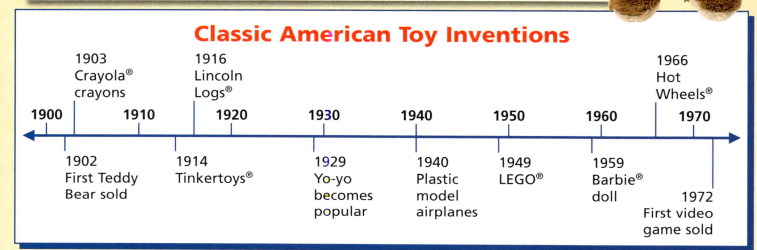

Classic American Toy Inventions

1903 Crayola® crayons
1916 Lincoln Logs®
1966 Hot Wheels®

1900 — 1910 — 1920 — 1930 — 1940 — 1950 — 1960 — 1970

1902 First Teddy Bear sold
1914 Tinkertoys®
1929 Yo-yo becomes popular
1940 Plastic model airplanes
1949 LEGO®
1959 Barbie® doll
1972 First video game sold

✏️ **WRITE HERE**

Read the time line and answer the questions.

1. What is this time line about?

2. Read the first and last date on the time line. What is the amount of time shown on the time line? Show your work.

3. Write a new title for this time line.

4. Which happened first, the invention of the Barbie® doll or the Teddy Bear?

© 2003 Options Publishing Inc.

NET CONNECTION
Make your own charts and graphs at http://www.smartdraw.com

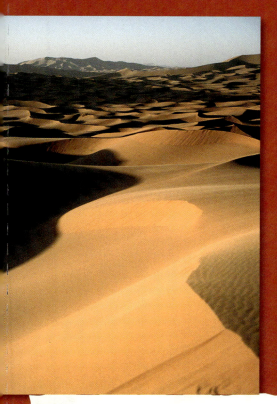

Rain Forests and Deserts

South America is home to the world's largest rain forest. It is a huge jungle. Africa is home to the world's largest desert. The native people on both continents know how to live in these difficult areas. They have done so for centuries. But times are changing. And so is their way of life.

Think About Comparing and Contrasting

When you **compare**, you tell how people, places, or things are alike. When you **contrast**, you tell how they are different. To compare and contrast, follow these tips:

- As you read, look for topics that have something in common. Topics are the people, places, or things you read about.

- Ask yourself: How are they alike? How are they different?

- Write the ways they are the same. Then write the ways they are different.

Think About the Topic

Reread the paragraph at the top of the page. On the lines below, write one way South America and Africa are different.

_____

_____

_____

_____

_____

_____

LESSON 5 — Comparing and Contrasting

STRATEGIES•TEST PREP
Question
Compare and Contrast
Recognize Point of View
Predict
Draw Conclusions
Use Study Skills

Question

Writers help you learn new facts by making connections or comparing and contrasting ideas with things you already know.

Rain Forests and Deserts

Life in the Rain Forest

The Amazon River starts its journey in Peru. It runs across Brazil until it spills into the Atlantic Ocean. Most of the river flows through a rain forest. Millions of unusual trees, plants, and animals live in the hot, steamy jungle. But you won't find many people here. Like the Sahara Desert in Africa, the rain forest in South America has a small population.

The native people were the first to settle in the rain forest. Some still live deep in the jungle. They follow old ways. Their homes are made of mud and dried palm tree leaves. They hunt with bows and arrows. For food, they also eat nuts, berries, and honey. They fish with nets or traps. These natives do not grow crops.

WRITE HERE

The author compares something about the Sahara Desert in Africa and the rain forest in South America. What does the author say is the same in both of these areas?

_____

© 2003 Options Publishing Inc.

Life Next to the River

Other native people also live in the rain forest. They live in communities next to the river. Because the river often floods, they build their wood homes on **stilts**. They grow crops, such as bananas, beans, or corn. The women find herbs for medicine.

People deep in the jungle and those next to the river use the river for fishing and travel. In their canoes, they take their goods to trade at markets.

Rain Forest Areas in South America

stilts long wooden poles sunk into the water to hold a building above the water.

Compare and Contrast

When you **compare** and **contrast**, you look at how things or ideas are alike and different. Comparing and contrasting helps you understand information in the article.

WRITE HERE

On page 54, you read about the natives who live deep in the rain forest. On this page, you read about those natives who live next to the river.

List one way that shows how the lives of the river people are different from the lives of the people living deep in the forest.

_____

Contrast Point of View

Point of view is a way a person looks at something based on his or her experiences, feelings, or ideas. The native people in the Amazon have their point of view about the forest. The Brazilians also have a point of view. List two ways that these feelings about the forest are different.

Danger to the Rain Forest

Hundreds of inches of rain fall in the forest every year. Most forests in the United States get only about 50 inches of rain or less.

The Amazonian Indians adapted well to this very wet climate. They take from the land only what they need to exist. They think of the forest as their own.

The government of Brazil does not think of the land as belonging to the natives. Brazilians want to use the many riches of the forest. Years ago they began to develop the land. Brazilians cut down or burned trees to make way for roads and farms.

Rivers now have dams to produce power. Miners drill for oil and iron ore. Tourists travel the Amazon. Cruise ships carrying tourists travel up and down the river.

The Indians are angry. These changes harm the forest. Rivers are polluted. Some types of wildlife have died out. Great areas of trees are gone. This has caused the weather to change. Now there is less rainfall.

The natives do not want any more trees cut down. The forest is a special place for them. They believe that every living thing has a spirit.

WRITE HERE

Amazonian Indians' point of view	Brazilians' point of view
1.	1.
2.	2.

Nomads in the Sahara Desert

The Tuareg (TWAH-reg) are a group of people who live in the Sahara Desert in Africa. These desert people are nomads. They move from place to place looking for food and water. They don't settle in one place for very long. The Sahara Desert is their only home. Like the natives of the Amazon, the Tuareg also believe that everything has a spirit.

Thousands of years ago, heavy rain fell in parts of the Sahara. Cave paintings show that large animals, like elephants and rhinos, used to roam in tall grasses. But over time, the Sahara changed. The climate, or weather, got hotter and hotter. Rivers dried up. Strong winds blew the sand. With no water, animals and plants died. The people who lived here had to learn to adapt, or change, to live in this new climate.

A Tuareg man travels with his camel.

Compare and Contrast to Predict

When you **predict** (pri-DIKT), you guess what will happen or how things will change. You have learned about life in the rain forest. Now you will read about life in the desert. To contrast these areas, think of some ways that a rain forest and a desert are different.

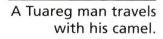
WRITE HERE

List two ways that you think the desert will be different from the rain forest.

1. _____

2. _____

LESSON 5
Comparing and Contrasting

oasis (oh-AY-siss) a small area of water in the desert where plants and trees grow. The water may be a pool on the surface or underground.

Compare and Contrast to Draw a Conclusion

Camels carry everything the people own. Camels travel without drinking water. Compare camels to other animals you know. You can **conclude** that camels are very important to the people.

The Tuareg stayed in the Sahara. They are called the princes of the desert. They raise camels and goats. Camels are useful in the desert. <mark>They can travel for days without drinking water.</mark>

<mark>The camels carry what little the Tuareg own.</mark> The families live in grass huts or tents. Both are easy to move. The tents are made of camel skin and dried grasses.

These nomads eat simple foods, like dried dates and bread. They drink goat's milk and mint tea. Their clothes are made of thin, cool fabric. The men cover their heads with blue or white veils. The veils protect them from the heat and dust.

Today, more Tuareg are settling in one place, usually at an **oasis**. An oasis has fresh water and rich land for crops. Nomads stop in these oases to rest. They trade their camels and goats for food.

Camels drink at the banks of the Nile River in Egypt.

WRITE HERE

The author says that more Tuareg are now settling at oases. Why do you think the nomads are settling at oases?

_____

_____

A camel caravan travels in the Sahara.

caravan
(KA-ruh-van)
a large group of people traveling together, often for protection. They travel to new places to trade goods.

The Caravans Disappear

In the past, the Tuareg were known for their trade **caravans**. The camels carried salt, cloth, and other products to markets. On the way back, the nomads brought gold and leather. These long trips could last for months. Caravans were an important business.

Like the lives of the Amazonian Indians, the lives of the nomads have changed. Roads now cut across the desert. Trucks carry goods where camels once walked. The Tuareg still run caravans, but not very many. Instead, they make cloth, knives, and swords to sell. They can no longer move as freely as before. More and more land is being developed or used for farming. There is less land for camels to graze.

The desert may look like a very difficult place to live. But it can be easily harmed. Scientists think the Sahara will become drier and hotter. It rains only about two inches a year, if that. Without rain, more land will turn to dust. The Tuareg may have to move away from the desert to survive.

Compare and Contrast the Past and Present

As you read, compare and contrast how the Tuareg used to live and how they live now. Have their lives changed? What caused their lives to change? Look for these facts as you read. Then answer the questions.

WRITE HERE

1. List two things that caused the Tuareg's way of life to change.

a. _____

b. _____

2. How has their way of life changed?

_____

_____

Compare Facts to Draw a Conclusion

Often you have to draw your own **conclusions** from the facts an author gives you. Think about the facts you have learned about the rain forest in this article. Compare how the natives and the Brazilians have used the rain forest. Then answer the question below.

Save the Rain Forest

The Amazon is also being harmed. Scientists say that without rain forests, the earth's weather may change. The earth will get hotter. Many people worry about how these changes will harm the earth. They now work to save the Amazon.

Brazilians admit they have made mistakes. Today, they are trying to save the rain forest. People are planting new trees in cleared land. Some factories and sawmills have shut down. Plans for new dams have been stopped.

Only time will tell if the way of life for the Amazonian tribes and the nomads of the Sahara can be saved. ■

Replanting trees in a rain forest.

 NET CONNECTION
http://passporttoknowledge.com/rainforest/main.html

WRITE HERE

After reading this article, why do you think the Amazon rain forest is worth saving?

_____

_____

_____

Compare and Contrast Pictures

A **primary source** is writing or drawings made by people who lived during an event. The people took part in or saw this event. Photographs, diaries and journals written at the time, and artwork are examples of primary sources.

Study the two pictures below. Then answer the questions.

These huts are built in the Tuareg village.

These houses are built on stilts along the Amazon River.

WRITE HERE

1. List two ways that the pictures are alike.

a._____

b._____

2. List two ways that the pictures are different.

a._____

b._____

© 2003 Options Publishing Inc.

Compare and Contrast Using a Venn Diagram

A **Venn diagram** is a good tool for comparing and contrasting information. The ways in which two things are alike are written in the middle, where the two circles overlap. Things that are common just to the Amazonian Indians are written on the left. Things common to the Tuareg are written on the right. Complete the Venn diagram by listing facts from the list below. Look back at the article if you need to check where to list a fact. The diagram is started for you.

Facts About Amazonian Indians and the Tuareg

- travel by canoe
- sell knives and cloth
- hunt with bows and arrows
- believe land is sacred
- drink mint tea
- build homes on stilts
- live simple lives
- live in homes made of grasses
- depend on animals to survive
- use herbs for medicine

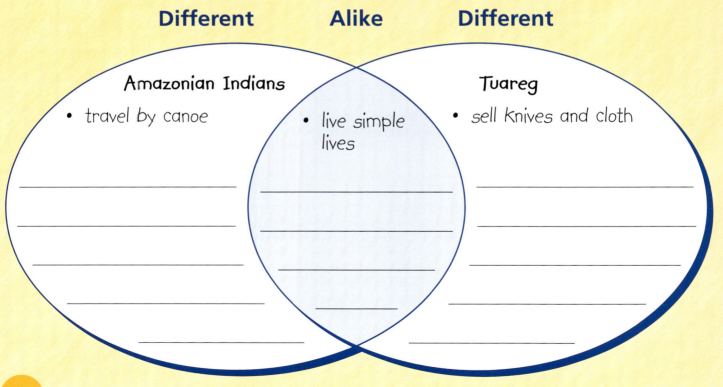

Different   **Alike**   **Different**

Amazonian Indians

- travel by canoe

- live simple lives

Tuareg

- sell knives and cloth

Compare and Contrast to Write a Summary

Nonfiction tells you about real people, places, and things. "Rain Forests and Deserts" is an article. It gives you facts.

To help you remember facts in an article, **write a summary**. In a summary, you tell only the most important things. You leave out many of the smaller details that are part of the article.

Write a short summary of "Rain Forests and Deserts." Use the list you made on page 62 to help you. In your summary, include the following:

- tell how the native people live in the Amazon

- tell how the nomads live in the Sahara

- tell how their lives are changing

Compare and Contrast to Write a Description

Pretend that a tribe from the Amazon has invited you to spend a few days living with them in the rain forest. After canoeing up the river, you step into the jungle. Think about what you would see and hear. On the lines below, compare the sights and sounds in your city or town with those of the rain forest. You may want to use ideas from the summary you wrote on page 63.

	Where I live	In the Amazon
What I *see*		
What I hear		

The City of Tokyo

Imagine living in one of the most populated cities in the world. Tokyo, Japan, was once a small sea town. The Japanese culture is thousands of years old. Tradition is an important part of Japanese culture. Tradition is the handing down of customs, ideas, and beliefs from one generation to the next. Today, Tokyo is a huge city. Millions of people live here. Buildings fill every street. But in this crowded city, things work smoothly.

Think About Fact and Opinion

As you read, you make decisions about the information you are given. To make good decisions, you must be able to tell the difference between a fact and an opinion.

• A **fact** is something that is true. *Millions of people live in Tokyo.* You can prove this is a fact by looking in a history book, an encyclopedia, or on the Internet.

• An **opinion** is what someone thinks, feels, or believes. An opinion is neither true nor false. *I think Tokyo is a beautiful city.*

Sometimes, opinions use words like *think*, *believe*, *good*, *love*, *bad*, *great*, *terrible*, or *beautiful*.

Think About the Topic

Reread the short introduction above for "The City of Tokyo." Write two facts that you learned about Tokyo on the lines below.

1. _____

_____

2. _____

_____

STRATEGIES•TEST PREP

Question

Tell Fact from Opinion

Recognize Point of View

Compare and Contrast

Use Study Skills

kimono

(kuh-MOH-nuh)
a long robe with
wide sleeves and
a wide sash.

Question

To find facts in an article, ask questions as you read. Use these questions to set purposes for your reading. These are some questions you may have about "The City of Tokyo."

The City of Tokyo

Tokyo is a crowded city. The city is on the island of Honshu, Japan. Mountains cover a big part of the island. The only flat land lies along the coasts. This is where the Japanese live, work, and farm. They make good use of small spaces in Tokyo.

Tokyo looks like any other big city. The capital of Japan has busy highways and fast trains. Neon signs light up downtown. There are many stores, businesses, and museums. Tokyo is a modern city. Yet they have very old customs. Most Japanese enjoy modern life. However, they may wear a **kimono** to work. Or they may go to an ancient tea ceremony. They blend the old customs with the new.

WRITE HERE

As you read, look for facts to answer these questions.

What does Tokyo look like?

What kinds of foods are popular in Japan?

Write a question that you hope to answer as you read about life in Tokyo.

_____

_____

Japanese Culture

Most Japanese share many of the same customs and beliefs. They speak the same language. To show respect, Japanese people bow to one another. The Japanese have wonderful **traditions**.

Some families in Tokyo have strict and traditional rules. Men work long hours at their jobs. Many women stay at home and care for the children. Some women do work outside the home, but as in many cultures, they are often not paid as much as men are. Children are taught to be polite and to respect others. Family is very important.

These women are wearing kimonos and greet each other by bowing.

> **tradition**
> the handing down of customs, ideas, and beliefs.

Tell Fact from Opinion

Facts can be proved. **Opinions** are what people think, feel, or believe. Look for words that show opinions: *good, bad, wonderful, happy, sad,* or *think*. Not all opinions include these words. Opinions are not right or wrong. They tell you what someone thinks.

WRITE HERE

Write one fact from the first paragraph. Then find an opinion in the same paragraph. Tell why you think it is an opinion.

Fact: _____

_____

Opinion: _____

_____

I think this is an opinion because

_____

_____

Use Fact and Opinion to Find Point of View

Point of view is a way a person looks at something based on his or her ideas, feelings, and experiences. The Japanese eat their food with chopsticks. For soup, they use chopsticks to pull out the noodles. Then they pick up the bowl and sip the broth. It is common to slurp the soup.

Life at Home

The Japanese eat rice, fresh vegetables, and fish. They often drink hot green tea with their meals. Noodle soup is also popular. Food is served on small dishes with chopsticks. Children learn to use chopsticks as young as the age of two. Children are taught that chopsticks should not be licked, waved in the air, or used to poke at food.

Many Tokyo homes are small and made of wood. Shoes are taken off and left in a

A young girl learns to use chopsticks.

hallway as people enter. Straw mats cover the floors. During meals, families sit on cushions at a low table. At night they sleep on futons. Futons are small mattresses that are put on the floor. In the morning, the futons are rolled up and put away in a closet. Homes have few pieces of furniture. That way, rooms can be used in many different ways. For example, a living room can also be a bedroom.

WRITE HERE

Think about the food you eat and the way you eat it. Could you eat your food with chopsticks? From your point of view, are forks, knives, and spoons easier or harder to use than chopsticks? Why do you think this is so? Explain your opinion.

_____

_____

Working in Japan

The Japanese love animals. But they may not have room in their homes for pets. Instead of owning a dog or cat, they sometimes rent one. Stores rent animals for a week or just a few hours. Some shops sell toy pets made of paper or wood.

The Japanese have invented many products. Cell phones and televisions are some of the products made in Japan. Japan's factories also make cars, machinery, and ships. Electronics are big **exports**. Some men and women spend long hours each day working in factories. Some people work six days a week. Tokyo companies treat their workers like family. But they have strict rules too. People must work in teams. They eat lunch and dinner together. They also go to parties and meetings after work. Loyalty and strong team spirit are important.

A Japanese worker at a telephone manufacturing factory.

exports (EK-sports) products sent to other countries to be sold.

Check the Facts
Articles are often found in newspapers and magazines. They explain a subject and contain many facts. Remember that **facts** are true. When you find a fact, make sure it can be proved or checked in a book.

WRITE HERE

List a fact on this page. Then tell where you would check to prove that it is a fact.

_____

_____

Learning and Having Fun

Going to school in Japan can be hard work. ==In Japan, the school year runs from April to the next March.== Classes are even held on Saturdays. Students learn both Japanese and English. They take difficult tests every year. When a child misses a day of school, his or her mother may go to school and take notes in class for her child. Children are taught

Japanese students are having a music lesson.

that good grades are important. ==No one likes to get poor grades!==

Children clean their own classrooms. If the school has a garden, they often weed and plant flowers. After school, they may take music or swimming lessons. Many also go to "cram schools." These schools help them do well on their tests. There is homework too. Students spend two to five hours a night studying.

Change Fact to Opinion

Facts can be proved. *In Japan, the school year runs from April to the next March.* **Opinions** are what someone thinks or believes. *No one likes to get poor grades!* You cannot prove what people like or dislike.

✏ **WRITE HERE**

Change this fact sentence to an opinion sentence. Underline the clue word in your sentence that makes it an opinion.

Students spend two to five hours a night studying.

_____

_____

The Japanese say **calligraphy** brings their words to life. Writing is an art. Children learn to write Japanese by first drawing the symbols in the air. On paper, they use brushes made of bamboo and black ink. They try to make each brush stroke strong and graceful. If they make a mistake, they cannot erase the black ink!

Learning to write Japanese symbols takes a long time. There are thousands of symbols. The symbols stand for a word or an idea. Japanese is written from top to bottom, instead of left to right. Writing Japanese is like painting a picture. Brushes are used, not pens. Each symbol must have the right number of brush strokes. Students practice calligraphy every day.

These Japanese symbols mean "river" or "stream."

Students brush ink on rice paper to make Japanese symbols.

calligraphy (kuh-LIG-ruh-fee) the art of handwriting that the Japanese began centuries ago.

Use Facts to Compare and Contrast

A good way to learn about people, places, or things is to compare and contrast them. When you **compare**, you tell how the people, places, or things are alike. When you **contrast**, you tell how they are different.

WRITE HERE

Think about how you first learned to write the alphabet. Did you use a pencil or a pen? Did you study handwriting every day? Explain how you learned to write.

_____

_____

_____

Find Facts in a Picture

This painting is a Japanese woodblock print. It was made about two hundred years ago. Children in Japan still learn this form of art today. Woodblock prints are made by carving a picture into wood. Ink is put on the wood. Then the wood is pressed onto paper. Woodblock prints are usually scenes from nature, daily life, or plays.

This woodblock print shows women writing a poem.

WRITE HERE

Look at the picture. What two things in the woodblock print are still used by the Japanese today?

1. _____

2. _____

Manga artists make colorful comic books.

Children have free time in Japan too. They like to play soccer, baseball, and video games. They also fly really beautiful kites and read comic books.

These comic books, called manga (mahn-GAH), can be as big as telephone books. There are comics about sports, hobbies, cooking, and more. Adults read comics too.

In a crowded world, the Japanese find quiet spaces. They hike and ski. They relax in hot springs. It is also great fun to visit gardens and see flowers in bloom.

Identify Fact and Opinion

You can prove a **fact** by looking in a history book, an encyclopedia, or on the Internet. An opinion cannot be proved. Look for words that signal an **opinion**: *think, feel, good, bad, terrible, great, love,* or *beautiful.*

WRITE HERE

Read each sentence below. Write **F** if it is a fact. Write **O** if it is an opinion. Underline the clue word if the sentence is an opinion.

1.____ They hike and ski.

2.____ There are comics about sports, hobbies, cooking, and more.

3.____ It is also great fun to visit gardens and see flowers in bloom.

4.____ They also fly really beautiful kites.

© 2003 Options Publishing Inc.

samurai
(SAM-oo-rye) a warrior who lived in ancient Japan.

temple (TEM-phul) a building used for worship.

Understand Fact and Opinion

Read the article about festivals. Look for **facts** and **opinions** as you read. Write two facts and two opinions from "Let's Celebrate."

Let's Celebrate

The Japanese have wonderful holidays all year. They celebrate the seasons. An important holiday is on New Year's Day. People clean their homes for the holiday. Old clothes and other things that are worn out are replaced. Debts are paid off. On New Year's Eve, they have a holiday feast. Then at midnight, bells ring out from the **temples**.

In spring, people make colorful kites for the kite festival. Spring is also the time to honor children. The Doll Festival is great fun. The girls dress up in kimonos. Friends come over to look at their dolls and to eat rice cakes. On Children's Day, boys display their **samurai** swords and warrior dolls. Many homes fly carp streamers on a pole. The carp is a fish that stands for strength and courage. ■

NET CONNECTION
http://www.jinjapan.org/kidsweb/

FACTS	OPINIONS
1. _____	1. _____
_____	_____
2. _____	2. _____
_____	_____

Compare and Contrast Facts

Photographs, like articles and stories, can show **facts** about a subject. Look at these two photos. One is an American living room. The other is a Japanese living room. On each side of the diagram, write the ways the two rooms are different. In the middle of the diagram where the two circles overlap, write the ways the two rooms are alike. The diagram is started for you.

Different   **Alike**   **Different**

American Room

couch

_____

_____

_____

_____

both living

space for families

_____

_____

_____

Japanese Room

no couch

_____

_____

_____

_____

Use Fact and Opinion to Write a Letter

Imagine that you have a new pen pal in Tokyo. He or she wants to know all about your daily life. Think about how different your life is from your pen pal's life. How would you describe your school and your home? What would you like your friend to know about your customs?

Write a letter to your pen pal. Include at least one fact and one opinion.

Dear _____ ,

_____

_____

_____

_____

_____

_____

_____

_____

_____

_____

_____

Your friend,

_____

Earth's Nearest Star

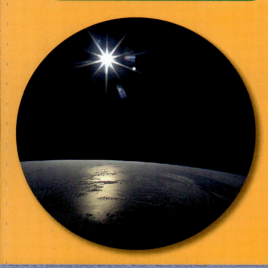

Did you know that the Sun is a star? It is the closest star to Earth. The Sun is important to Earth. Have you ever wondered why Earth has seasons? It is the movement of Earth around the Sun. Without light and warmth from the Sun, there would be no life on Earth.

Think About Main Idea and Supporting Details

The **main idea** tells what the paragraph or story is mostly about. **Supporting details** describe or explain the main idea.

- Look for the most important idea. That is the main idea.

- Look for facts and examples about the main idea. They are the supporting details that help you understand the main idea.

- Titles, pictures, and maps all help you understand the main idea.

Main Idea:
The Sun is important to Earth.

↓

Supporting Detail:
The movement of Earth around the Sun causes the seasons.

Think About the Topic

Look for main ideas and details as you read. They will help you remember what you read.

Read the paragraph at the top of this page. Look at the headings and pictures in the article on pages 77–88. Now predict, or guess, what the main idea is for this article. What will it be mostly about? Write your prediction below.

_____

_____

_____

_____

_____

_____

_____

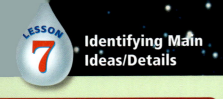

LESSON 7
Identifying Main Ideas/Details

STRATEGIES•TEST PREP

Question

Identify Main Idea/ Supporting Details

Understand Cause and Effect

Draw Conclusions

Use Study Skills

solar system
the Sun and the group of planets, moons, asteroids, and other objects that circle it.

Question

As you read, ask questions. Tell the main idea in your own words. Then find the details.

The main idea is that the Sun is important to Earth. I'll look for details that support, or tell me about, the main idea.

Earth's Nearest Star

What do you see when you look up at the sky on a cold, clear night? The dark sky is filled with stars. In the daylight, you can still see a star. It is the Sun. The Sun is our daytime star. The other stars are still there. But we cannot see them because the Sun is so bright. The Sun is about 93 million miles from Earth.

==The Sun is a very important star in our **solar system**. It keeps us warm and gives our planet light and energy.==

You can't look at the Sun the same way you look at other stars. The Sun is so bright that it can harm your eyes, or even cause blindness.

Scientists use powerful telescopes, spacecraft, and satellites to learn about the Sun. Telescopes collect light and send back to Earth pictures of objects far away. Spacecraft carry cameras and computers that send back pictures to scientists. Satellites are spacecrafts sent into space to circle Earth or other planets.

WRITE HERE

List two details that explain how scientists study the Sun.

1. _____

2. _____

© 2003 Options Publishing Inc.

78 Level C • Lesson 7

Hot Topic: The Sun

<mark>The Sun is a bubbling ball of hot gases.</mark> When these gases erupt, or blow up, they shoot thousands of miles into space. The Sun began as a cloud of gases at the edge of the **Milky Way**.

Two gases make up the Sun. One gas is called hydrogen (HYE-druh-juhn). The other gas is called helium (HEE-lee-uhm). The Sun burns these gases to produce energy. Tons of hydrogen gas burns every second on the Sun. As the gases burn, they make energy. This energy makes heat and light.

The temperature on the surface of the Sun is about 10,000 degrees Fahrenheit. Inside the Sun, the temperature can get as hot as 27 million degrees Fahrenheit.

On some parts of the Sun, the gases cool down. When they cool, the gases become dark spots. We can see them from Earth. Scientists call these dark areas sunspots. These spots are cooler. They give off less light and heat.

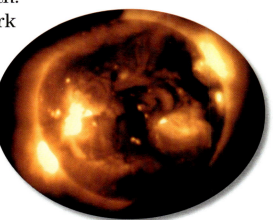

Sunspots are dark areas on the Sun's surface.

Milky Way
a band of billions of stars. It is seen as a hazy white streak across the night sky.

Understand Main Idea

In this part of the article, you learn about the Sun. The **main idea** of the first paragraph says that "The Sun is a bubbling ball of hot gases." Read to find out details about the Sun.

WRITE HERE

1. What gases does the Sun burn?

a. _____   b. _____

2. How do these gases produce heat and light?

_____

_____

orbit (OR-bit)
the path followed by an object circling a planet or circling the Sun.

Identify Main Idea and Details

Details are important. They give you more information about the **main idea**. Look at the main idea web. The main idea is in the middle circle. As you read about our solar system, list two details in the blank ovals that support the main idea.

Our Solar System

The Sun is the center of our solar system. Planets and moons travel around the Sun. Asteroids (AS-tuh-roids) and other objects in our solar system also travel in circles around the Sun.

There are nine planets in our solar system. Each planet follows its own **orbit** around the Sun. The four planets closest to the Sun are called the inner planets. They are Mercury, Venus, Earth, and Mars.

Scientists call this asteroid 243 Ida. Ida is 35 miles long.

The four outer planets are called Jupiter (JOO-puh-tur), Saturn (SAT-urn), Uranus (yu-RAY-nuhss), and Neptune (NEP-toon). These are giant planets made of gases. Scientists sometimes call these planets the gas planets. The ninth planet, Pluto (PLOO-toh), is the farthest from the Sun. Pluto is very small.

Between the inner and outer planets is a belt of asteroids. Asteroids are made of smaller bits of rock and ice.

Detail

Main Idea

The Sun is the center of our solar system.

Detail

Understand a Diagram

A **diagram** is a drawing or a plan that explains how things work. The title tells the main idea of a diagram. Study the diagram below. It shows the objects in our solar system and how they move around the Sun. Then answer the questions.

Our Solar System

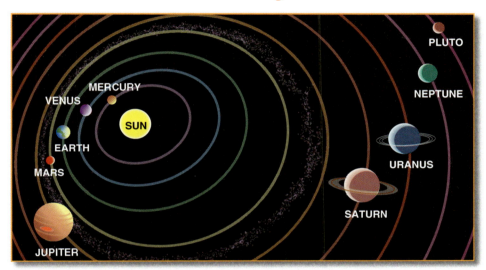

1. What is the main idea of this diagram?

_____

2. What is the name of the planet that is the closest to the Sun?

_____

3. Why do you think Pluto is the coldest planet? Explain your answer.

_____

_____

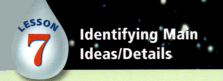

axis (AK-siss)
an imaginary line
through the middle
of Earth, around
which Earth spins.

Use Details to Find Cause and Effect

Often, supporting details explain what makes something happen. The reason something happens is the **cause**. What happens is the **effect**. Because Earth itself spins around as it circles the Sun (cause), we have day and night (effect).

How the Earth Moves

Earth moves around the Sun in two ways. First, it rotates, or spins around and around itself, like a wheel. Earth rotates on an imaginary line called an **axis**. The axis runs through the center of Earth from the North Pole to the South Pole. It takes twenty-four hours for Earth to spin completely around on its axis.

The movement of Earth spinning on its axis causes day and night. It makes the Sun appear to rise and set at a certain time every day. One side of Earth faces the Sun. As a result, that side has daylight. The side of Earth that is opposite the Sun's light is in darkness.

The Earth Rotates As It Orbits the Sun

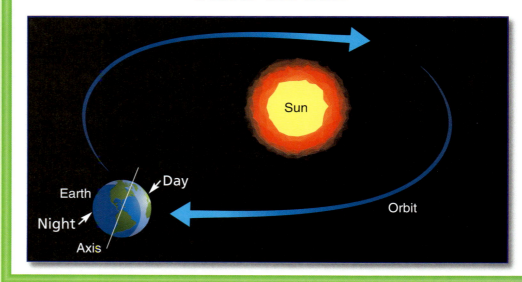

WRITE HERE

Study the diagram and read the paragraph.
Then complete the chart.

Why?/Cause	What Happens?/Effect
One side of Earth faces the Sun.	As a result, that side has _____

As Earth spins on its axis, it also travels around the Sun. It takes one year for Earth to orbit the Sun.

During Earth's orbit around the Sun, parts of the world have winter and summer at different times of the year. This is because Earth **tilts** on its axis.

Imagine living in New England and going to the beach during the winter. In the southern half of the world, that is possible. When the North Pole tilts toward the Sun, the northern half of Earth has summer. At that time, it is winter in the southern half of the world. While people in North America are enjoying summer, people in Australia are having winter. Winter is cooler than summer because there is less light and heat from the Sun.

tilt to lean or tip; an angle that is not straight up and down.

Use Details to Support a Conclusion

When authors draw **conclusions**, they include facts and details to support the conclusions: "Winter is cooler than summer because there is less light and heat from the Sun." Look for details that support this conclusion.

The Seasons

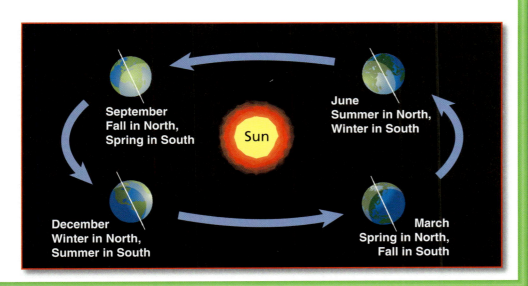

September
Fall in North,
Spring in South

June
Summer in North,
Winter in South

Sun

December
Winter in North,
Summer in South

March
Spring in North,
Fall in South

WRITE HERE

List one detail that supports, or explains, the author's conclusion: "Winter is cooler than summer because there is less light and heat from the Sun." Use the diagram to help find the answer.

_____

_____

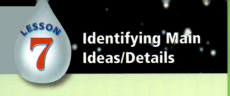

Find Supporting Details

Supporting details can help you understand the main idea by giving you more information about the main idea. Always explain the details using your own words. This will help you remember the most important ideas.

The Land of the Midnight Sun

There are people called the Inuit (IHN-yoo-it) who live in the Arctic North. These areas are northern Canada, Alaska, and Greenland. The word *inuit* means "real people." They were once called Eskimos. The Inuit live farther north than any other people in the world.

Imagine seeing the Sun at midnight. The Inuit live in the area called "the land of the midnight sun." At the North Pole, the Sun does not set for six months. From about March 20 to September 23, the Sun shines 24 hours every day. When the Sun shines all day, it is called the midnight sun.

The midnight sun is caused by the tilt of Earth's axis as it travels around the Sun. When one pole tilts toward the Sun for six months, the other pole tilts away from the Sun. That pole receives no sunlight. At the South Pole, the Sun shines 24 hours a day from about September 23 to March 20. This is the opposite time of year from the North Pole. ■

The midnight sun shines over the Arctic Ocean.

NET CONNECTION
http://starchild.gsfc.nasa.gov/docs/StarChild/solar_system_level1/solar_system.html *and* http://kids.msfc.nasa.gov/

 WRITE HERE

Explain why the sun shines 24 hours a day for six months of the year at the North Pole. Use details from the paragraph. Write your answer using your own words.

_____

_____

_____

Understand Details Using a Map

The **map** below shows details about the Arctic region of Earth. It helps you understand where the North Pole and Arctic Circle are located. Use the map to answer the questions.

Arctic Region of Earth

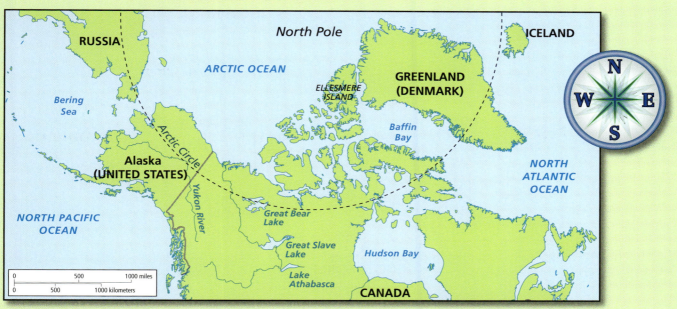

WRITE HERE

1. Find the Arctic Circle. Name the countries that spread into the Arctic Circle.

a. _____   c. _____

b. _____   d. _____

2. At the North Pole during April, there are about 720 hours of sunlight. In the United States during April, there are about 390 hours of sunlight. How many more hours of sunlight are there at the North Pole? Show your work.

_____

_____

Main Ideas and Web Map Details

A **web map** can help you understand main ideas and supporting details. The main idea is written in the center circle. Complete the map by writing in details that support the main idea. The map is started for you.

Detail:
Causes day
and night

Detail:
Causes the
seasons

Main Idea:
Earth spins and
moves around Sun

Detail:
Explain how

_____

_____

_____

_____

Detail:
Explain how

_____

_____

_____

_____

Use Main Ideas and Details to Write a Summary

Nonfiction gives you information about real people, places, and things. "Earth's Nearest Star" is a nonfiction article. It gives you facts about our solar system and our nearest star, the Sun.

To remember these facts, **write a summary**. Use your own words to tell the most important ideas in the article. Use the web map on page 86 to help you write part of this summary.

In your summary, include the following:

- tell why the Sun is called our daytime star
- tell why the Sun is hot
- tell how Earth moves around the Sun

© 2003 Options Publishing Inc.

Write Interview Questions

Authors often include interviews when they write articles. Imagine that you were asked to write an article about Inuit children. What questions would you ask the children about their lives?

Use the information you learned about the land of the midnight sun to ask **interview questions**. Write four questions you would like to ask Inuit children about their lives.

My Interview Questions

1.

2.

3.

4.

A Reason to Celebrate

People all over the world love to celebrate. Some holidays remember special events in history or religion. Some days honor special people. Other holidays celebrate special times of the year. There are holidays for harvest time or the beginning of a new year. Holidays tell stories about cultures. They tell about the way a group of people lives and their customs.

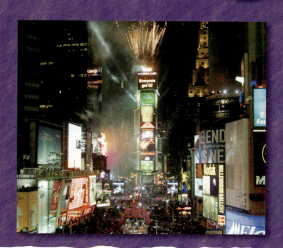

Think About Classifying

When you **classify**, you put things or ideas into groups. You can classify, or group, ideas, living things, and objects. Classifying helps you understand better the things you put into groups. Look at the chart. It shows you how you can classify some items.

Objects	Classify into Groups
truck, bus, car	Things that have wheels
bat, airplane, bird	Things that fly

To classify, follow these tips:

- Study the items. Think about how they are alike and different.
- Make groups that show how some of the items are alike.

Think About the Topic

Reread the paragraph at the top of this page. It tells you the different reasons why people celebrate. Use what you already know about some holidays to classify them. Write the holiday from the list below its correct group.

Fourth of July

Martin Luther King, Jr.

New Year's Eve

Type of Holiday:

Special People

_____

Special Event in History

_____

Special Time of the Year

_____

STRATEGIES•TEST PREP
Question
Classify
Compare and Contrast
Identify Main Idea/
Supporting Details
Use Study Skills

A Reason to Celebrate

Special Times of the Year

Question

Ask questions as you read. Change each heading into a question using *Who*, *What*, *When*, *Where*, *Why*, and *How*. This helps you classify information as you read.

The first heading becomes:

What are the special times of the year?

The streets crowd with people. People wear costumes or play music. All cultures celebrate special times of the year. We have spring festivals, fall harvests, and big parties for a new year.

In most places in the world, the weather changes as the seasons change. In the Northern Hemisphere, hot summer passes into cool fall. Crops have been growing all summer. Now they are ready to be gathered, or harvested. Fall is a special time of year for many people around the world.

Harvest festivals date back to when people first began to grow their own crops. To these people, a good harvest was a matter of life or death. A good harvest in fall meant your family and community lived through the winter.

WRITE HERE

Read the first paragraph of "Special Times of the Year." What special times of the year do people celebrate?

1. _____

2. _____

3. _____

© 2003 Options Publishing Inc.

The early Greeks and Romans held fall festivals. People gave thanks to their gods that the crops were good. These parties had music, games, and sports. There was also a huge feast. Many countries throughout Asia also have harvest festivals.

Harvests and Moon Cakes

Long ago in China, people used the moon to tell them when to plant and harvest crops. In the fall, people celebrated the moon's birthday. Special cakes made from the harvested rice were baked. They were shaped to look like the full moon. Bright lanterns lit up the night.

In many places in Asia, this festival is still celebrated. In modern-day China, families still go outside to enjoy the full moon. They light candles in lanterns. They eat round or fish-shaped moon cakes made of rice.

In Singapore, a country in Asia, people hold the Feast of Lanterns. Dancers lead a parade through the streets. Music is everywhere. Behind the dancers, other people hold up a dancing dragon held high on bamboo poles.

In Vietnam, people also light candles in lanterns. They wear masks as they parade down the streets. What is one of the favorite foods? Moon cakes. They are shaped to look like fish.

Moon cakes in the shape of fish are served as treats at Asian moon festivals.

Understand Classifying

When you **classify,** you group things together that have something in common. Read "Harvests and Moon Cakes." Then answer the question.

WRITE HERE

List two things that many Asian countries have in common at the harvest festivals.

1. _____

2. _____

Classify Past and Present

You can classify some events as past or present. **Past events** happened before today. **Present events** are happening now. Look for facts on this page about Thanksgiving in the past and today. Look for key words, such as *today* or *long ago*. Look for dates. Key words and dates help you classify events.

An American Thanksgiving

Today, Thanksgiving in America is special. It is a time for families to get together. Many people have a feast of turkey, stuffing, cranberry sauce, potatoes, and pumpkin pie.

Giving thanks began long ago with the first Pilgrims. In 1620, the Pilgrims landed in America. It was winter. They had little food. The Native Americans helped the Pilgrims. They taught the Pilgrims to plant crops and to hunt.

Thanksgiving is a time for family and friends.

The next fall, the Pilgrims thanked the Wampanoag (wahm-puh-NOH-agh) for their help. They feasted on wild turkeys, ducks, and deer meat. Two hundred years later, President Abraham Lincoln made the last Thursday in November Thanksgiving Day.

But giving thanks was not special to just the Pilgrims. Native Americans celebrated the harvest long before the Pilgrims landed.

In the fall, natives performed a Green Corn Dance. They gave thanks for the crops. Bread and corn soup were served. The feast went on for days.

WRITE HERE

Classify the information in the sentences. Write **Past** or **Present** after each sentence.

1. Today, Thanksgiving in America is special. _____

2. Giving thanks began long ago with the first Pilgrims. _____

3. In 1620, the Pilgrims landed in America. _____

An African Thanksgiving

The ten-year-old boy is nervous. He gets into his costume made of animal skins. This year, he will dance at N'cwala (enc-WAH-la). N'cwala is a special time for the Ngoni (na-GO-nee) people. They live in Zambia (ZAM-bee-a), in Africa. The Ngoni people celebrate to give thanks for their good harvest.

The chief and his royal party travel to the N'cwala. The chief is offered the first fruits and vegetables from the harvest. Then he watches the ceremony. On a field, twelve groups of dancers take turns performing a warrior dance. Parts of their outfits are made of animal fur. The chief chooses one group as the best warrior dancers. At their feast, all the people eat corn and beef stew.

Men dancing at N'cwala.

Compare and Contrast to Classify

When you **compare**, you tell how people, places, or things are alike. When you **contrast**, you tell how they are different. Think about how an African and an American Thanksgiving are the same and how they are different. Then complete the Venn diagram below.

WRITE HERE

List one fact under each heading about an American and an African Thanksgiving.

Different   **Alike**   **Different**

American   African

_____   _____   _____

_____   _____   _____

_____   _____

LESSON 8 — **Classifying**

Classify and Compare

It is important to understand what you read. It helps to think about what you already know about a subject. Think about how you celebrate New Year's Day. **Classify**, or group, the events you know about. Read this page and answer the question below.

A Special Time of Year: The New Year

Five. Four. Three. Two. One! Fireworks shoot into the air. People laugh, blow horns, and sing. It is the start of another new year. You may have seen the huge, shiny New Year's Eve Ball in Times Square in New York City. The ball is lowered down a pole as the seconds are counted down. When it reaches the ground, the New Year has begun.

New Year celebrations take place in most parts of the world. For many people, a new year means a new start in life.

One of the most colorful New Year celebrations is the Chinese New Year. Chinese communities all over the world celebrate. It is a time to feast and visit with family. Chinese families clean their houses to get rid of last year's bad luck.

Many people wear red clothing. Red is the color for joy and happiness. There is a huge parade. People dressed as dragons and lions dance their way through the streets.

✏ WRITE HERE

List one thing that happens during the Chinese New Year. Then list one thing that happens during your New Year celebration.

Chinese New Year	Your New Year
_____	_____

Are they alike or very different? How?

_____

_____

In Iran, the New Year is called Nawruz (no-ROOZ). It means "new day." The holiday lasts for thirteen days. People spend the last day with family and friends. Some take picnics to the countryside. Clowns, dancers, and singers perform in the parks.

Most cultures celebrate the new year. Jewish communities have Rosh Hashanah (rush-uh-SHAH-nuh). The Vietnamese New Year is celebrated with fireworks and drums. In Denmark, young people throw old plates and cups against their neighbors' doors! Wherever New Year's Day is celebrated, it is a time for family and friends.

A new year also brings new promises. People decide to exercise more or lose weight. Some people decide to spend more time on homework. People put the past behind and begin a new year.

This colorful dragon is part of a Chinese New Year parade.

Identify Main Idea and Supporting Details

The **main idea** is the most important idea in a paragraph. Always look for **details** that support, or explain, the main idea.

WRITE HERE

The main idea of this paragraph says that "A new year also brings new promises." List two details in the paragraph that give you examples to help explain the main idea.

1. _____

2. _____

Understand Classifying

When you **classify**, you group things together that have something in common. Classifying helps you understand and remember information. Read this page. Then answer the questions.

Too Important to Forget

Most countries have holidays celebrating special events in their history. They may mark the day when a nation was born, or when it won freedom from foreign rule. Some countries remember a famous battle.

Can you guess this holiday? It's summertime. People are at picnics. Everyone is excited about the fireworks. In fact, there will be fireworks going off across the United States. Yes, it's the Fourth of July. We celebrate the day the American colonies said they would no longer be ruled by England.

Cinco de Mayo, May 5, is Mexico's day to remember winning freedom from France in 1861. Now, every year on Cinco de Mayo, Mexico holds street fairs and parades. Musicians and dancers wear colorful costumes. People sing and dance to folk music. Mexican communities in the United States also celebrate.

Dancers at a Cinco de Mayo parade.

WRITE HERE

1. What event does Cinco de Mayo celebrate?

   _____

2. List one way that Cinco de Mayo and the Fourth of July are alike.

   _____

   _____

Bastille Day is a national holiday in France. It begins July 14th with a one-hundred-cannon salute. Then, a grand parade starts. People dress in red, white, and blue, the colors of the French flag. Everywhere there is music and dancing. At night, fireworks explode in the sky. It is the day the French celebrate their freedom and liberty from the rule of kings.

A fireworks display celebrates Bastille Day.

Special People

Countries also celebrate special people. Many cultures have special days honoring mothers, fathers, and children. Other holidays honor people who helped their countries.

In America, a holiday honors Martin Luther King, Jr. He fought for civil rights and freedom for all people. George Washington and Abraham Lincoln are two of the best-loved American presidents. Their birthdays are celebrated as holidays.

Compare and Classify

When you read about several events, look to see if they have some things in common. **Compare** the events. Then see if you can **classify**, or group, what they have in common.

WRITE HERE

1. Compare Bastille Day and the Fourth of July in the United States. List two ways these holidays are alike.

a. _____   b. _____

2. Think about President Abraham Lincoln, President George Washington, and Martin Luther King, Jr. List one thing that all three of these men had in common.

_____

© 2003 Options Publishing Inc.

Find Details in a Picture

Have you ever heard someone say, "One picture is worth a thousand words." It means that sometimes a **picture** can explain things better than words can. Study the details in the picture. Then answer the questions.

There is even a holiday in Japan to honor dolls called Hina Matsuri (Hee-na mat-SOO-ree). Nearly every Japanese girl owns a set of special, beautiful dolls. Many are very old. They are put in the best room in the house. These dolls are to look at. They are not to play with. Special dolls are put into boats. The boats are put into the sea. Some people believe that the dolls take away bad luck.

No matter who we are or where we live, we love to celebrate. People around the world celebrate special days, people, and times of the year. ■

This Japanese family celebrates Hina Matsuri.

NET CONNECTION
http://www.yahooligans.com/around_the_world/Holidays

WRITE HERE

1. What is the picture about?

_____

_____

2. What is the woman in the picture doing?

_____

_____

Understand How to Classify Information

Charts help you classify information. Study the lists of words about holidays below. They are words that appear in this lesson. Look through the article to find the words. Then classify the words by the type of holiday. Fill in the columns to complete the chart.

Cinco de Mayo   Nawruz

N'cwala   Feast of Lanterns

Fourth of July   George Washington

Abraham Lincoln   Martin Luther King, Jr.

Rosh Hashanah   Bastille Day

Special People	Special Times of Year	Special Events in History

Write an Invitation

Think about what you have learned about the different types of holidays. Think about why people celebrate holidays. Imagine that you are sending a friend an **invitation**. You are inviting this person to join you to celebrate one of your holidays. On your invitation, write a short paragraph that describes the holiday you choose.

Join Me to Celebrate

_____
(name of holiday)

This holiday celebrates

_____

_____

_____

_____

_____

Dear _____,

Please come help me celebrate!

Who: _____
(your name)

When: _____

_____

Where: _____

_____

Hope you can join me.
We will have fun!

Understanding Documents

A document (DOK-yuh-muhnt) is something that is written or printed. Photographs, diaries, letters, maps, and drawings are examples of documents. They give you information or facts about an event. To understand what a document means, you must look carefully at the details and read all of the words.

Think About Documents

You create documents all the time. When you write a letter or take a picture with your camera, you make a document. These documents are called **primary sources** because they are **firsthand** records of what you saw or did. A primary source is a document that people make about something they do or an event they see happen.

When a person writes a book or draws a picture about an event that happened long ago, it is a **secondhand** document. These documents are also called **secondary sources**. A secondary source is a document that someone makes about an event that happened long ago. The person was not present during the event.

To understand documents, ask yourself the **5Ws** and **H**:

- **Who** are the characters or people in the document? **Who** will read or see the document?

- **What** is the document about? **What** do I already know about the subject of the document?

- **Where** and **when** was it made? **Why** was the document made?

- **How** does the document help me understand what happened?

Think About the Topic

Use the information from **Think About Documents** to complete the sentence. Circle the letter of the correct answer.

A photograph that you took of your school at track and field day is a

A. primary source document.

B. secondary source document.

Question

To understand
documents, ask
yourself questions.
Read the titles
and captions. Ask
yourself: *What is
this document
about? What does
it show me?* Look
for details that
answer the **5Ws**
and **H.**

Understanding Documents

Understand Posters

Posters are printed signs that often have pictures. A poster can tell you about something you need to know. It can also be a decoration or an advertisement.

Artists give clues to help you understand what the poster is about. Read the title and words. Look for symbols. A **symbol** is an object that stands for something else. For example, think of Uncle Sam. He has a white beard and wears a tall hat. He is a symbol for the United States. In the poster on the next page, Smokey the Bear is a symbol for fire prevention (pri-VENT-shun). He reminds people to prevent, or stop, forest fires.

Follow these tips to help you understand posters:

- Think about the subject. What event or idea is the poster about? Study the characters. Who are they and what are they doing?
- Read the title and all the words. They tell you what the artwork is about. Look for dates or clues that tell you when the artwork was done.
- Look for symbols. What do the symbols stand for?

I WANT YOU
FOR U.S. ARMY
NEAREST RECRUITING STATION

✏️ **WRITE HERE**

Study the poster on the opposite page.
Then answer the questions.

1. What do the words tell you?

_____

2. What does the bear stand for?

_____

The Real Story About Smokey the Bear

A national park is land that is set aside for people to enjoy. Forest fires are a problem in most national parks. Fires kill trees, plants, and animals. Trees burn and animals lose their homes.

Many fires start because people are careless. Some people are careless with matches, or they do not make sure their campfires are put out. It is the job of the United States Forest Service to protect America's national parks.

In 1950, there was a terrible fire in New Mexico. A bear cub was hurt in the forest fire. The forest rangers saved the bear. His story was printed in the newspapers. People across the country read about the little bear. They learned about the problem of forest fires. After doctors helped the cub get well, he was sent to a new home at the National Zoo in Washington, D.C.

Because people fell in love with the little cub, the forest service decided to use a bear to teach people about fire prevention. They drew a bear and called him Smokey. They made the bear a park ranger. They used the poster of Smokey to remind people to be careful about forest fires.

This poster teaches people about outdoor fire safety.

✏️ **WRITE HERE**

Study the poster. Read the words and then answer the questions.

1. Look at the bear. What does his hat tell you about his job?

_____

_____

_____

2. The poster says that "only you can prevent forest fires." How can you prevent, or stop, these fires?

_____

_____

_____

Look for the Main Idea

Remember to ask yourself questions about the poster. Think about the subject and look for details. Ask yourself: *What is the main idea of this poster? Are there any symbols that stand for something else? What are the characters doing?* Study the travel poster on the next page. Then answer the questions below and on the next page.

Understand an Advertising Poster

Some posters are used as advertisements. An advertisement is something that tells about a product or a service. Artists give clues to help you understand the meaning of a poster. Look for clues in the title and words, in the symbols used, and in the details.

The poster on the next page is called a travel poster. The travel company that made it wants people to take a trip to Egypt. The Sphinx (SFINGKS) is a famous monument found in the desert of Egypt. It was carved out of limestone thousands of years ago. The figure has the head of a human and the body of a lion. The Sphinx guards the pyramids, which are the tombs of the ancient Egyptian kings.

People from all over the world travel to Egypt. They want to see these ancient treasures. The Sphinx and pyramids have become symbols for Egypt. When people see these treasures, they think of Egypt.

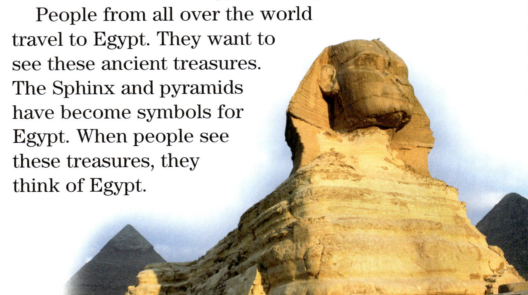

WRITE HERE

1. What is the title of the poster on page 105?

_____

2. List the people and objects you see in the poster.

_____

_____

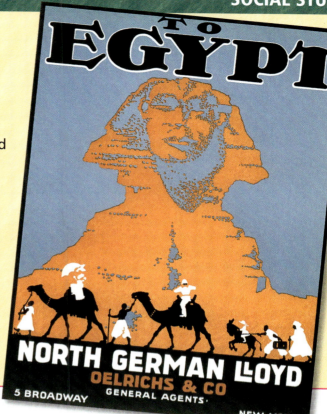

This poster was created in the 1930s. The travel company wanted this poster to convince people to sign up with their company for a trip to Egypt.

WRITE HERE

1. What details in the poster tell you that this part of Egypt is a desert?

_____

_____

2. Why does one person carry an umbrella?

_____

_____

3. Why did the artist create this poster?

_____

4. Imagine that you are making a travel poster for your city or town. What place, object, or person would you put on your poster? Why?

_____

_____

_____

election day
a day when people go to a special place and elect, or vote for, their leaders.

Recognize Point of View

A person's **point of view** is his or her opinion. It is the way a person looks at something based on his or her feelings, ideas, or experiences. Artists have a point of view. By looking at the cartoon, you can see how they feel about a subject.

Understand Political Cartoons

Political cartoons are drawings. They make people think about events that are happening now. Artists draw political cartoons to tell their point of view, or opinion, about an event in the news. They sometimes use words and symbols in their artwork. Follow these tips to understand political cartoons:

- Study the cartoon. Think about the subject. What event or idea is the cartoon about?
- Study the characters. How are they dressed? What are they doing?
- Read the title and all the words. They tell you what the cartoon is about. Identify objects in the cartoon.
- Look for symbols. Are the people or objects symbols that stand for something else?

The cartoon on page 107 is called "**Election Day**." It was published on January 21, 1909. At that time, women were working to get the right to vote.

Many people thought it was wrong for women to vote. They believed that families would fall apart. They thought that women would no longer take care of the children.

Finally, on August 24, 1920, Congress passed the nineteenth amendment to the Constitution. This amendment gave women the right to vote. ■

✏️ **WRITE HERE**

Look at the cartoon on page 107. Complete the chart.

People: Who are the people? How are they dressed?	Activities: What are the people doing?

Understand Political Cartoons

This **political cartoon** shows what some men imagined might happen if women were allowed to vote.

Look at the cartoon again. Use the chart you completed on page 106 to help you answer the questions below.

WRITE HERE

1. What is the title of the cartoon?

_____

2. What does the sign on the wall say?

_____

3. Look at the man's face. How do you think he feels?

_____

4. What does the artist think might happen if women get the right to vote? What details support your answer?

_____

_____

_____

Understand Photographs

Photographs tell us about people, places, and events. Photographs tell a story without words. Follow these steps to understand photographs:

- Study the photograph. What is the subject or main idea? What is happening in the picture?

- Carefully look at the people, objects, and activities. If there are people in the photograph, ask yourself what they are doing. Try to guess when the photograph was taken. You can often guess the date by the subject. Or look at how they are dressed.

- Ask yourself what story the photographer is telling you.

The photograph on the next page shows a Hopi (HOH-pee) buffalo dance. The Hopi live in northeastern Arizona. In 1921, Edward S. Curtis took this photograph of a buffalo dance.

The Hopi needed the buffalos to survive. They used the skins for clothing and ate the meat. Every year they did a special dance to make sure there would be many buffalo for the hunt.

Think about the story the photograph tells. Then complete the chart below.

People: Who are the people? How are they dressed?	Activities: What are the people doing? Why are they there?

Hopi people celebrate the importance of the buffalo to their lives.

WRITE HERE

Look at the photograph. Use your completed chart to answer the questions.

1. This photograph was taken in 1921. What details in the photograph help you know that this photo was taken a long time ago?

_____

2. What are the people doing in the photograph?

_____

_____

3. List two things that you see dancers wearing in the photograph.

a. _____

b. _____

4. Why do you think the photographer thought it was important to take this picture?

_____

_____

Compare and Contrast Using Photographs

When you **compare**, you tell how people, places, or things are alike. When you **contrast**, you tell how they are different. You can compare and contrast details in **photographs**. Details in each part of a photograph give you information and facts about the subject or topic. They give clues that tell you where and why a photographer took the picture. Details help you understand how things are alike and how they are different.

Study the two photographs on page 111. Then complete the chart below.

Photograph:	Rain Forest Bridge	Mountain Bridge
What are the people and animals doing?		
What kind of environment do you see?		
What does the photograph tell you about how people live and travel?		

Villagers and animals walk along a mountain bridge at sunset in China.

People travel across a rope bridge in the rain forest of Costa Rica, a country in Central America.

✏ WRITE HERE

Study the photographs and use your chart to answer these questions.

1. Imagine you are crossing these bridges. Describe what you see as you cross each bridge.

a. Costa Rica _____

_____

b. China _____

_____

2. Do you think travel is easy or difficult for people in both photographs? Explain your answer.

_____

_____

_____

Find Details in a Photograph

People in the Bahamas have a festival called Junkanoo (JUNK-ah-noo). Junkanoo was started by African slaves in the 1700s. At that time, slaves were allowed to visit with their families around Christmastime.

Today, people celebrate Junkanoo with colorful parades. The people in the parades wear beautiful costumes. They play flutes and whistles. Other people beat drums. They all dance down the main street. Everyone joins in the fun.

Study the photograph. Then answer the questions.

WRITE HERE

1. Write one detail from the photograph that tells you this is a special event.

_____

2. List two activities that are happening in the photograph.

a. _____

b. _____

 NET CONNECTION
http://www.kidinfo.com/American_History/HistoricalEvents.html
and http://www.smokeybear.com/

© 2003 Options Publishing Inc.

Insect Communities: Ants and Bees

You learned that people form communities. Did you know that ants and bees also form communities? Some insects work together to help their community survive. Scientists know that ants and bees are social insects. They are part of an insect community that works together.

Think About Taking Notes

When you **take notes**, you organize information. Notes help you understand what you are reading. Here are some steps to follow to take good notes:

- Quickly look through the article to see what it is about. Think about *what* you are reading *while* you are reading. This is called **active reading**. Ask the **5Ws and H** as you read: *who, what, when, where, why,* and *how.* Your notes are the answers to these questions.

- Use your own words in your notes. Use just a few words instead of complete sentences.

- Don't worry if you have trouble pronouncing names and other hard words. Don't try to pronounce the word each time you read it. If you do, you may forget what you are reading about. Read to get the main ideas and supporting details.

Think About the Topic

Reread the paragraph at the top of the page. Quickly look through the article on pages 113 to 124. What do you think this article is about?

_____

_____

_____

_____

When you take notes, look for the main idea and supporting details. Notes help you remember what you read. Read what you just wrote. You wrote your first note.

LESSON 10 — Taking Notes

STRATEGIES•TEST PREP
Question
Take Notes
Identify Main Idea/
Supporting Details
Make a Cluster Map
Identify Sequence
Use Study Skills

Question

Notes help you understand details about science. Details tell you the *who*, *what*, *when*, *where*, *why*, and *how*. Remember to ask yourself questions about the **5Ws and H**. As you read, write down the answers to your questions. Here is an example of what your notes should look like.

Insect Communities: Ants and Bees

Three Kinds of Ants in the Colony

Ants are social insects. They live and work together in a community. An ant community is called a colony. In an ant colony, every ant is important. Each has a special job to do. These jobs are important to the success of the colony.

Inside a colony, there are three kinds of ants. Each kind is a different size. The biggest ant is a female called the queen. The queen has only one job. She lays eggs. The second biggest ants are males. Their job is to mate with the queen. The smallest ants in the colony are the worker ants. Worker ants are also female, but they do not lay eggs.

What are the three kinds of ants in a colony?

- queen
- males
- workers

Helpful Hint
Notice that the "notes" information on this page is highlighted.

© 2003 Options Publishing Inc.

114 Level C • Lesson 10

Worker Ants Have Many Jobs

Worker ants have many different jobs. Some hunt for food for the colony. Others clean and care for each egg, **larva**, and **pupa**. Still others take care of the queen. Some ants dig tunnels. Others guard and defend the colony.

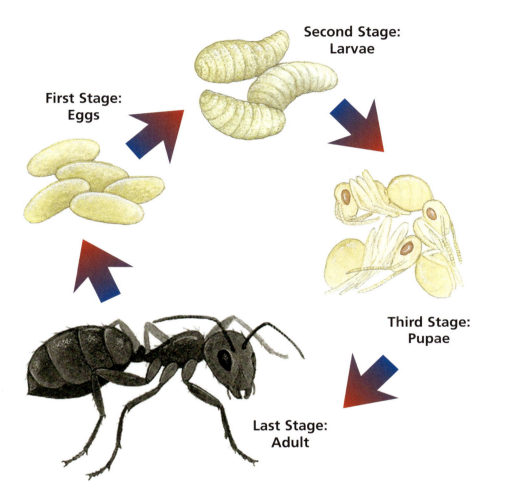

First Stage: Eggs

Second Stage: Larvae

Third Stage: Pupae

Last Stage: Adult

larva (LAR-vuh) the second stage of an insect's life, between an egg and a pupa when it looks like a worm.

pupa (PYU-puh) the third stage of an insect's life, between a larva and an adult.

Take Notes

Now it's your turn to take notes from the article. Write a *short* **note** that answers the questions below. Don't use complete sentences. Use your own words.

WRITE HERE

1. Explain who lays eggs for the ant colony.

_____

2. Who hunts for food?

_____

LESSON **10**

 Understand a Diagram

A **diagram** is a drawing or a plan that explains or shows information in a picture. Diagrams help explain how things go together or how they work. The title tells what the diagram shows.

This diagram of an ant colony shows some of the jobs that worker ants do.

Worker Ants Have Many Jobs

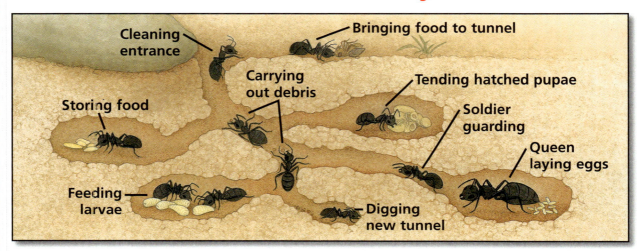

Study the diagram and think about what you have learned about worker ants. Then answer the question.

List four jobs that worker ants do for the colony.

1. _____

2. _____

3. _____

4. _____

© 2003 Options Publishing Inc.

Ant Talk

These ants use their antennae to communicate.

==For the colony to survive, the ants must communicate or "talk" to one another.== Ants use touch, taste, and smell to communicate. When ants meet, they touch each other with their antennae (an-TEN-ee), or feelers, on top of their heads. This is the way that ants gather information and pass it on.

Each ant learns about another ant by smell and taste. They know where the ant has been, what it has been doing, and even what type of job it has in the colony.

When worker ants find food, they return to their nest. They want the other ants to know where to find the food. Ants leave a trail of scent, or smell, that marks the way to the food. The other ants follow the trail to the food.

If you have ever watched a line of ants marching along, you can bet that they are following a scent. They are either leaving or returning to their nest.

Take Notes Using Main Ideas

The **main idea** is the most important idea. It tells you who or what you are reading about. When you take notes, the first thing you write is the main idea. Read this page. The main idea is highlighted. Think about the main idea. Then answer the question below.

WRITE HERE

For the colony to survive, the ants must communicate or "talk" to one another. List two details that explain why it is important for ants to talk to one another.

1. _____

2. _____

© 2003 Options Publishing Inc.

Busy as a Bee

Bees also live in communities. Like ants, bees are social insects. Each bee depends on the community to survive. Many types of bees live in hives.

The largest bee in a hive is the queen bee. Her job is to lay eggs. The queen bee can lay as many as 1,500 eggs in one day. The male bees are called drones (DROHNS). They mate with the queen bee.

There are many jobs in a hive. Most of the bees in a hive are female worker bees. Worker bees keep the hive clean. They also guard and defend the hive. Some workers care for the eggs, larvae, and pupae. Other workers look for and gather food. Some workers have the job of caring for the queen. Honeybees also make honey. They use the honey for food.

Two bees make honey inside a honeycomb.

Take Notes Using Supporting Details

Supporting details help explain the main idea. Good notes include details that tell you more about the main idea. Read "Busy as a Bee." Look for main ideas and supporting details.

WRITE HERE

Read this main idea sentence. Then list three ideas that support, or tell more about, this main idea.

Main Idea: There are many jobs in a hive.

1. _____

2. _____

3. _____

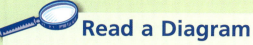

Read a Diagram

Below is a diagram that shows the inside of a beehive. Look at the notes you made about bees on page 118. Then study the diagram.

Inside a Beehive

WRITE HERE

1. Describe three jobs that are being done in the beehive.

a. _____

b. _____

c. _____

2. How do these jobs help the bee community survive?

_____

_____

_____

Take Notes Using 5Ws and H

Science articles are filled with facts that answer some of the questions *Who*, *What*, *When*, *Where*, *Why*, and *How*. As you read "The Honeybee Dance," look for facts that answer some of these questions. You will use this information on the next page when you make a cluster map. The first answer is highlighted for you.

The Honeybee Dance

Like ants, bees communicate, or talk, with each other to survive. Bees talk through sight, smell, and touch. Each queen bee has a special scent. Her hive and her worker bees are marked with that scent. Bees know if another bee is from their hive or from a different hive just by smell.

==Bees also communicate through a bee dance.== The bee does a round dance when food is close to the hive. The bee tells other bees about the flowers it has found. It tells them where the flowers are and if it has found many or very few. The faster it dances, the closer the flowers are to the hive.

This bee performs the round dance. The other bees learn where the flowers are. Then they zoom out of the hive to find the food.

WRITE HERE

1. What is "The Honeybee Dance" about?

_____

2. When do bees dance?

_____

3. Why do they dance?

_____

_____

Take Notes Using a Cluster Map

A good way to organize ideas and information is to make a cluster map. **Cluster maps** help you identify the main idea. They also help you find supporting details.

Fill in the cluster map for the part of the article called "The Honeybee Dance." The main idea is written in the center. Fill in the blank shapes with details that tell more about the main idea. The map is started for you.

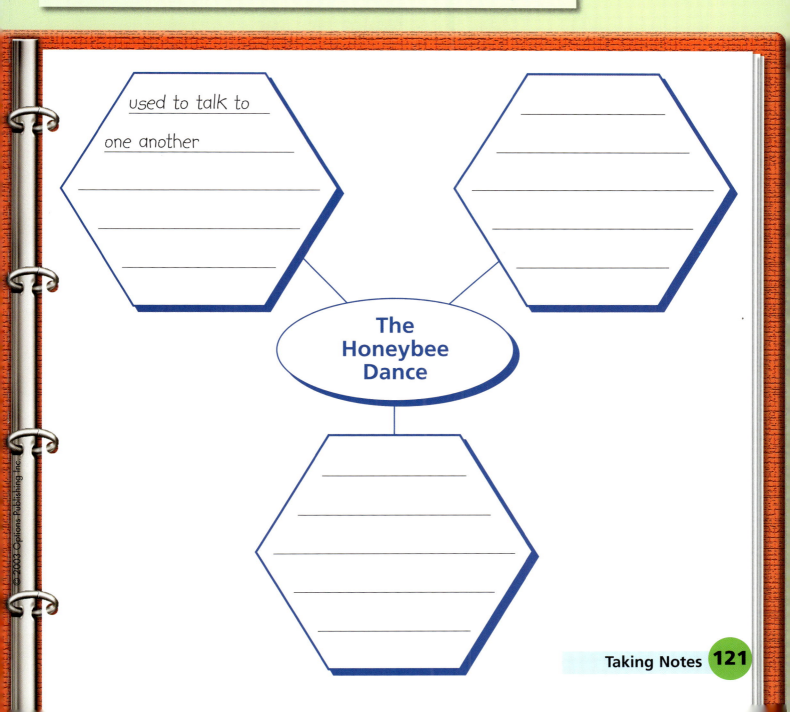

used to talk to one another

The Honeybee Dance

Take Notes Using Sequence

Learning to put things in order, or **sequence**, helps you understand many kinds of writing. In articles about history, sequence tells you the order of events. You look for dates. In science, you use sequence to tell you the correct steps in a process. Look for words that signal sequence, such as *first*, *then*, *next*, and *finally*.

A bee sucks nectar from a flower.

How Bees Make Honey

Honeybees make honey out of nectar. Nectar is a sweet liquid found deep inside a flower. First, bees land on flowers. Bees use their long tongues to suck the nectar from a flower. Then, they bring it back to the hive. At the hive, special workers chew the nectar. Only these workers have the special "honey stomach," where honey is produced.

Next, the worker bees spread the honey in the cells of the honeycomb and wait for it to dry. As it dries, the nectar gets very sticky. Finally, it turns into honey! The bees use this honey for food. People use the honey for food too. ◼

NET CONNECTION
http://www.infowest.com/life/aants.htm

✎ WRITE HERE

1. What is the first step in making honey?

_____

2. What is the last step in making honey?

_____

Take Notes by Making a Flowchart

A **flowchart** shows the correct order of steps in a process. It usually has arrows to show which step comes next. Flowcharts can help you take notes when you need to know how something works.

Reread "How Bees Make Honey" on page 122. Then complete the flowchart below.

How Bees Make Honey

bee lands on flower

Take Notes About "Insect Communities: Ants and Bees"

Use this page to take notes about "Insect Communities: Ants and Bees." First, look at all the headings in the article. Turn each heading into a question. Leave space between each question for your notes. Keep your notes very short. The questions are already done for you. Write your notes under each question.

1. **What are the three kinds of ants in a colony?**

   queen/ males/ workers

2. **What kinds of jobs do worker ants have?**

   _____

   _____

3. **How do ants talk to one other?**

   _____

   _____

4. **Why are bees so busy?**

   _____

   _____

5. **What is the honeybee dance?**

   _____

   _____

6. **How do bees make honey?**

   _____

   _____

Part 1 Multiple-Choice Test

Directions for Questions 1–13:

This part of the test has 13 multiple-choice questions. Each question is followed by four answer choices, labeled A through D. Read each question carefully. Decide which choice is the correct answer. Use a pencil to fill in the circle that has the same letter as the answer you have chosen.

Read the **sample question** below:

Sample Question

Each star on the American flag stands for a

Ⓐ state.

Ⓑ colony.

Ⓒ senator.

Ⓓ country.

The correct answer is **state**, which is next to the letter **A**. Fill in the circle that has the letter **A**.

Answer all 13 questions on Part 1 of this test. Fill in only one circle for each question. Be sure to erase completely any answer you want to change. You may not know the answers to some of the questions, but do the best you can to answer each one.

When you have finished Part 1, go on to Part 2.

Now begin Part 1 of the test.

Base your answers for questions 1 and 2 on the map below.

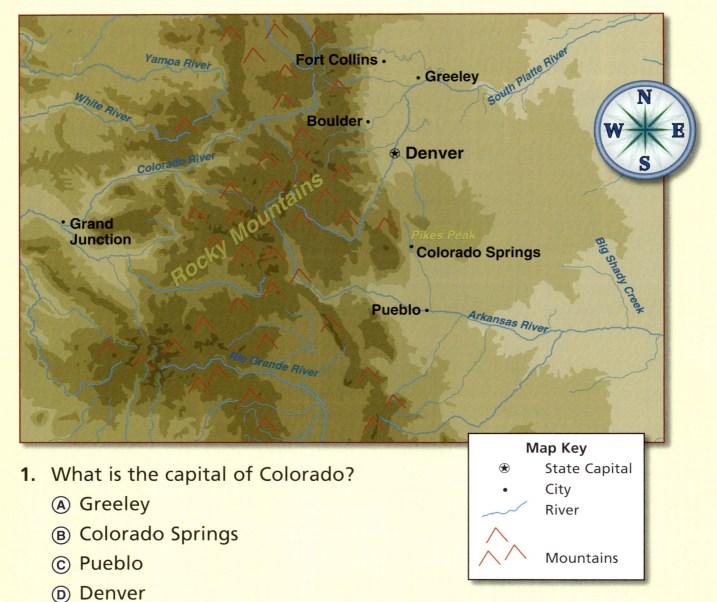

Map Key

✪	State Capital
•	City
〜	River
⋀⋀	Mountains

1. What is the capital of Colorado?

   Ⓐ Greeley

   Ⓑ Colorado Springs

   Ⓒ Pueblo

   Ⓓ Denver

2. In which direction would you travel if you left Greeley for Colorado Springs?

   Ⓐ north

   Ⓑ south

   Ⓒ east

   Ⓓ west

3. Because environments around the world are not the same,

   Ⓐ people live in the same way.

   Ⓑ people live in different ways.

   Ⓒ people build the same kinds of houses.

   Ⓓ people grow the same kinds of crops.

4. Rice grows best in hot areas with a lot of rain. Which continent has areas that are best for growing rice?

   Ⓐ Antarctica

   Ⓑ Australia

   Ⓒ Africa

   Ⓓ Asia

5. At the North Pole, the midnight sun does not set for the six months between March 20 and September 23. *Midnight sun* means that the sun

   Ⓐ shines 24 hours every day.

   Ⓑ never shines.

   Ⓒ shines for only one hour every night.

   Ⓓ only shines during the winter.

Base your answers to questions 6 and 7 on the circle graphs below.

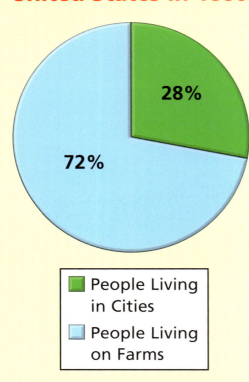

United States in 1880

28%

72%

▪ People Living in Cities

▫ People Living on Farms

United States in 2000

2%

98%

▪ People Living in Cities

▫ People Living on Farms

6. In 1880, most people lived
   Ⓐ in apartments.
   Ⓑ in cities.
   Ⓒ on farms.
   Ⓓ in towns.

7. Which statement is the best conclusion when you compare the two circle graphs?
   Ⓐ Most people like living on farms.
   Ⓑ The number of people living on farms is increasing.
   Ⓒ The number of people living on farms is decreasing.
   Ⓓ Cities do not have any jobs for people.

8. Which of the following is an example of a firsthand, or primary, source in which the author saw the event?

   Ⓐ a diary made by a Civil War soldier

   Ⓑ a make-believe story about a Native American child

   Ⓒ a chapter in your history book

   Ⓓ a drawing of a dinosaur

9. Which statement is an opinion?

   Ⓐ Tokyo is a city in Japan.

   Ⓑ Tokyo is the most beautiful city in Japan.

   Ⓒ The Japanese often wear kimonos.

   Ⓓ Millions of people live in Japan.

10. Early people were called hunters and gatherers because

   Ⓐ they traveled to find and collect food in the wild.

   Ⓑ they settled on the land and farmed it.

   Ⓒ they traveled to find water.

   Ⓓ they started farms and raised animals.

11. Compare and contrast the Sahara Desert with the rain forests of Brazil. The Sahara Desert

   Ⓐ gets more rain per year.

   Ⓑ has more trees.

   Ⓒ is much drier.

   Ⓓ has more animals.

12. The "honeybee dance" tells other bees

Ⓐ where and how many flowers a bee has found.

Ⓑ that it is time to return to the hive.

Ⓒ when the hive will be attacked by other bees.

Ⓓ what time food will be at the hive.

Base your answer to question 13 on the words in the box.

Title: _____

Thanksgiving

Feast of Lanterns

N'cwala

13. Which is the best title for the words in the box above?

Ⓐ New Year Holidays

Ⓑ Presidents' Holidays

Ⓒ Spring Holidays

Ⓓ Harvest Holidays

Go on

Part 2 Constructed-Response Test

Directions

Write your answers to the questions that follow on the lines in this book.

Base your answers for questions 1 and 2 on the photograph to the right. It shows fishermen in Myanmar (MYAHN-mahr), a country in Asia. You learned about how people travel and live in their environment in Lesson 1.

1. List two types of transportation that people in this Asian community use. [2]

   a. _____

   b. _____

2. Write one reason why the river is important to the people in this community. [1]

   _____

   _____

Base your answers to questions 3 through 5 on the map of the rain forests in South America on the next page. To answer the questions, use the map and what you learned about maps in Lesson 2.

South America has the largest tropical rain forest in the world. It is called the Amazon Rain Forest. It covers nine countries on the continent of South America. Study the map on the next page and answer the questions below.

3. Look at the map. Name the ocean on the west coast of South America. [1]

_____

4. What object on the map shows the four directions? [1]

_____

5. Which country has the largest area of tropical rain forest? [1]

_____

Tropical Rain Forests of South America

Base your answers to questions 6 through 8 on the diagram below and your knowledge of science. The diagram shows the life cycle of an ant. You learned about ants and bees in Lesson 10 of this book.

Use the diagram to answer the questions.

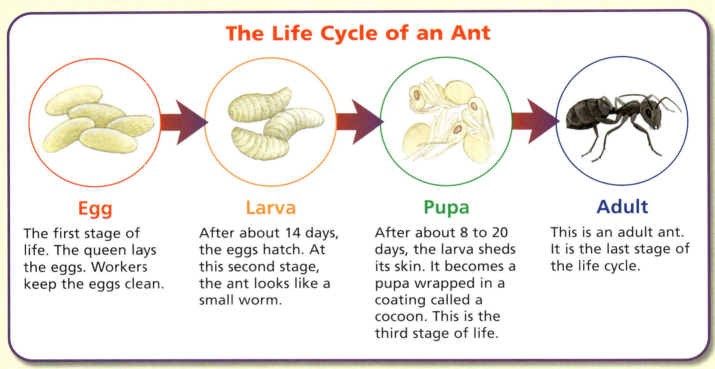

The Life Cycle of an Ant

Egg
The first stage of life. The queen lays the eggs. Workers keep the eggs clean.

Larva
After about 14 days, the eggs hatch. At this second stage, the ant looks like a small worm.

Pupa
After about 8 to 20 days, the larva sheds its skin. It becomes a pupa wrapped in a coating called a cocoon. This is the third stage of life.

Adult
This is an adult ant. It is the last stage of the life cycle.

6. What is this diagram about? [1]

_____

7. Which stage comes after the larva stage? [1]

_____

8. Describe the difference between the larva stage and the pupa stage. [1]

_____

_____

Stop

Part 3 Document-Based Question Test

Directions

The task below is based on Documents 1 through 4. This task tests how you work with documents.

Background

The Inuit live in northern Canada. It is very cold. There are no trees. The climate is too cold to grow crops. The people hunt and fish for food. Animals, such as seals, polar bears, foxes, and whales, are important. The Inuit use animals for food, clothing, and homes. The people use the skin and fur of animals to make warm clothing and blankets for their homes. They also use animal skins for tents and canoes.

The Inuit use sleds to travel over snow. They train dogs to pull the sleds over long distances. When people hunt or travel by water, they use special canoes called kayaks (KYE-aks). The Inuit learned to use things from nature to live in their arctic environment.

Task

Part A: Short-Answer Response. This part of the test has four documents. Study each document carefully. Then answer the questions following the documents. These answers will help you write your paragraph.

Part B: Paragraph. Use the information from the documents, your answers to the questions in Part A, and your knowledge of social studies and science to plan and write a paragraph.

- In your paragraph, explain how the Inuit use things from nature to help them live in their arctic environment. Think about what kinds of clothing they wear, what they eat, and how they travel over land and water.

Part A Short-Answer Questions

Directions: Study each document carefully. Then answer the questions that follow each document on the lines below.

Document 1

This drawing shows an Inuit igloo village around 1871.

The Arctic has few trees for wood. Long ago, the Inuit built dome-shaped houses called igloos. They used sealskin to cover the doorways. Igloos kept villagers safe from the bitter weather and dangerous animals.

1. Look at the drawing. What did the Inuit use to build their homes? [1]

_____

Document 2

An Inuit hunter stands in front of his tent at a summer hunting camp.

The Inuit use animals and fish for food. They also make jackets, hats, mittens, and boots from the skin and fur of animals. The clothing keeps them warm and dry. They use sealskins to cover the frames of tents and canoes so that water will not get inside. Polar bear skins make warm blankets and rugs for their homes.

2. What do the Inuit use to make tents and clothing? [1]

_____

_____

3. Look at the details in the photograph. List one thing from nature that the Inuit use to help them live. [1]

_____

Document 3

An Inuit hunter stops to rest beside his kayak.

An Inuit traveler calls to the dogs that pull his sled.

4. Look at each photograph on this page. List two ways that the Inuit travel in their environment. [2]

   a. _____

   b. _____

5. List one thing from nature that the Inuit use to keep warm. [1]

   _____

Document 4

An Inuit villager
fishes on a lake.

6. Look at the details in this photograph. How do fish help
    the man and his family survive? [1]

    _____

    _____

7. How might fishing in the Arctic be different from fishing in
    a warmer climate? [1]

    _____

    _____

 **Part B**

Paragraph

Directions: Write a paragraph using the information in the documents, the answers to the questions in Part A, and your knowledge about how the Inuit people live. Use the space below to make your notes.

Notes

_____

_____

_____

_____

Task: In your paragraph, tell how the Inuit use things in nature to help them live in their arctic environment. Be sure to include details about

- what kind of clothing they wear.
- what foods they eat.
- how they travel over land and water.

Write your paragraph on the lines below.

_____

_____

_____

_____

_____

_____

_____

GLOSSARY

Boldfaced words within the definitions are other terms that appear in the glossary.

 C

caption   a short title or description. It is printed below or next to a political cartoon, photograph, or drawing.

civilization   a highly developed and organized **society**.

climate   the yearly pattern of average temperatures, rainfall, winds, and hours of sunlight in an area.

colony   land that has been settled by people from another country. The colony is controlled and run by that country. A colony is also a large group of insects that live together, such as ants and bees.

community   a group of people who live in the same area or who share the same interests.

compass rose   a symbol on a map that shows directions: north, east, south, and west.

continent   one of the seven large landmasses of the earth. The seven continents are Asia, Africa, Europe, North America, South America, Australia, and Antarctica. A helpful way to remember the continents is that five of the continents begin and end with the same letter: Asia, Africa, Europe, Australia, and Antarctica. The other two include the word "America": North America and South America.

culture   the common way of life, ideas, customs, and traditions. These are shared by a group of people. Their culture may include a common language.

 E

environment   the natural world of the land, sea, and air.

equator   an imaginary line around the middle of the earth. It is halfway between the North and South poles. The equator divides the earth into the Northern and Southern **Hemispheres**.

 G

globe   a round model of the earth.

 H

hemisphere   one half of the globe. See **equator** and **prime meridian**.

 L

landforms   the different shapes that make up the earth's surface. Some of these landforms include mountains, plains, rivers, and islands.

latitude   imaginary lines that run east and west on a map or globe. These lines give the position of a place on the earth. The **equator** is a line of latitude.

longitude   imaginary lines that run north and south on a map. These lines give the position of a place on the earth. They are measured in degrees east or west of a line that runs through the Greenwich Observatory in England. Lines of longitude are drawn on a map or globe from the North Pole to the South Pole.

M

map key   also called a map legend. The key shows the meanings of the map symbols.

P

physical map   a map that shows major natural features, or **landforms**. Some of these landforms include mountains, rivers, or plains.

planet   one of the nine heavenly bodies circling the sun.

political map   a map that shows how people have divided up the earth's surface. This kind of map shows borders between **states** or countries.

primary source   materials or information written or made by people who lived during the time that an event occurred. See **secondary source**.

prime meridian   an imaginary line around the earth. It runs north and south through Greenwich, England. The prime meridian divides the earth into the Eastern and Western **Hemispheres**.

S

secondary source   materials or information about an earlier time or event. Secondary sources are written or made by people who lived in a later time. See **primary source**.

society   all the people who live in the same country or area and share the same laws and customs.

state   political and geographical units that make up a country. The United States has 50 states.

symbol   a design or an object that stands for something else. For example, a heart often stands for love. A dove stands for peace.

T

tradition   a custom, a belief, or an idea that is handed down from one generation to the next.